Mental Health
PLAYBOOK

A Journal
For Athletes

Luc Swensson

Mental Health Playbook
A Journal for Athletes

Copyright © 2026 by Luc Swensson
All rights reserved.

Thank you for purchasing an authorized
edition of this book and for
complying with all copyright laws.

For more information about using
parts of this book for
commercial use, or to contact the author
for insights or appearances,
please contact the publisher at:
ryan@thegetitfactory.com

ISBN: 978-1-953011-20-6

Drocus Ink
An imprint of:
The Get It Factory
In association with:
WYNX: A Content Company

Salt Lake City, UT

MENTAL HEALTH PLAYBOOK

A Journal for Athletes

HELLO and welcome

Welcome to the Mental Health Playbook and Thank you for being here. Over the next 52 weeks you will hear from former and current athletes in many different sports and what they have done to get over struggles in their careers. This isn't just a notebook, it's a space to track your progress, reflect on your journey, set bold goals, and unlock the mindset of a champion.

Whether you're chasing a personal best, recovering from a setback, or simply showing up with consistency this journal is here to support you.

Use it to celebrate your wins (big or small), and turn challenges into stepping stones. Greatness isn't just built on game day it's built in the quiet moments of dedication, discipline, and self-reflection.

> **OWN YOUR JOURNEY.**
> **RESPECT THE GRIND.**
> **TRUST THE PROCESS.**

Welcome to the team. You can do this, I believe in you!

-Luc

how to use this journal

This journal is your personal training ground for the mind. Just like you practice skills, build strength, and study your sport, you can also train your mindset. The pages ahead are designed for you to check in every day and help you stay focused, understand yourself better, and build the mental habits that lead to real growth, on and off the field.

You'll see different sections throughout the journal, each with a clear purpose. Use them regularly, and be honest with yourself. This is your space. No grades, no filters, just your story, your growth, your game.

Here's how it works:

Daily Prompts keep you consistent. A few lines a day can make a huge difference over time.

Weekly *Reflection Pages* are there after every week for you to look back and see how far you've come.

Monthly Themes give you a big-picture focus. Each month has a new skill or mindset to work on, like confidence, leadership, or resilience.

Mental Reps and Challenges are sprinkled in to push your thinking. These are like bonus workouts for your brain.

Use it at your own pace, but the more consistent you are, the more you'll get out of it. If you miss a few days, no problem. Just pick it back up. This isn't about being perfect. It's about showing up.

Set Some Goals

As you prepare for the time you have before your season really takes off, take some time to think about what you want from your sport. Not just wins or stats, but who you want to become.

Use this section to set clear, meaningful, long term goals. These goals are your foundation for the work ahead. You'll have a lot of short term goals, but these ones are for the big picture. Where do you want to be athletically this time next year?

These goals can help you stay motivated when things get tough and give you something to celebrate when you make progress.

Start with these three areas:

Athletic goals:
What do you want to accomplish this year in your sport? Think about your skills, mindset, and how you want to contribute to your team.

Personal Goals:
Who are you outside of sports? What habits, routines, or relationships do you want to improve?

Mindset Goals:
How do you want to respond when things don't go your way? What kind of mental toughness do you want to build?

Tips for setting strong goals:

Be specific. "Get better at defense" is good. "Cut down opponent scoring by 5 points per game" is better.

Make it measurable. You should know if you're on track.

Make them achievable. Winning the wrestling state championship in the heavyweight division is a great goal, but if you weigh 105 lbs, it might not be all that realistic for this one year period.

Add your long term goals on the next pages. Revisit them often, and add updates when you have them.

LONG TERM GOALS

1

UPDATES

2

UPDATES

3

UPDATES

4

UPDATES

5

UPDATES

MONTHLY Themes

Each month, this journal will guide you through a different mental skill. These are like focus areas for your brain. Habits and tools that help you handle pressure, lead with confidence, and stay locked in when it counts.

Here's an overview of what's ahead:

Month 1: Awareness
Start strong by learning how to check in with yourself. Notice your thoughts, moods, and patterns. Awareness is the first step in mental strength.

Month 2: Focus
Train your ability to tune out distractions and dial in on what matters. This month helps you build routines and concentration strategies.

Month 3: Resilience
Learn how to bounce back from mistakes, losses, and criticism. Develop the mindset to stay in the fight when things get hard.

Month 4: Confidence
Discover what true confidence looks like, and how to build it from the inside out. No fake hype. Just real belief in your work.

Month 5: Teamwork
Explore what it means to be a great teammate. Communication, connection, and accountability all matter.

Month 6: Grit
Grit is passion and perseverance over time. This month will stretch your endurance and help you push through mental fatigue.

Month 7: Leadership
You don't have to be the loudest or the oldest to lead. Leadership is about example, energy, and presence. Step up.

Month 8: Adaptability
Sports don't always go as planned. Neither does life. Learn how to adjust quickly and stay calm under pressure.

Month 9: Vision
Look ahead with purpose. What kind of athlete and person do you want to be six months from now? A year? Set your sights.

Month 10: Gratitude
You'll play better and live happier when you notice what's good. Gratitude doesn't make you soft...it makes you strong and grounded.

Month 11: Self-Talk
The voice in your head matters. Train it to be your biggest supporter, not your harshest critic.

Month 12: Reflection
Finish the year strong by looking back. Celebrate what you've accomplished and build momentum for what is coming next.

WRITE DOWN ANY THOUGHTS, CONCERNS, EXPECTATIONS, OR QUESTIONS YOU HAVE ABOUT THE MENTAL PERFORMANCE JOURNEY YOU'RE ABOUT TO UNDTERTAKE.

MONTH 1
Awareness

What is Awareness?

Awareness is the foundation of mental performance. It's about noticing what's happening in your body, mind, and environment, all without judgment. Athletes who work to understand awareness are better at adjusting in real time, staying calm under pressure, and bouncing back after mistakes. When you understand how your thoughts, emotions, and reactions work, you gain control over your performance instead of letting it control you.

Awareness is not just about noticing problems. It's about noticing growth, noticing patterns, and knowing when to push or pause. It shows up in the huddle, on the bench, during recovery, and in every moment of preparation.

This month, we'll hear from *Rob Schulte*, a former Gatorade Player of the Year and University of Montana standout, who built his game (and now his life) on awareness, humility, and preparation.

Meet the Athlete:
Rob Schulte

Rob Schulte grew up in Montana and made his name as one of the state's most decorated high school football players, earning the Gatorade Player of the Year honor in 2003. He went on to play wide receiver for the Montana Grizzlies, where his work ethic and leadership helped lead the team to three Big Sky Championships and a national title game appearance. Known for his humility, toughness, and mental sharpness, Rob was also named Scout Team Player of the Year during his redshirt season—an award that reflected his mindset of showing up fully even when the spotlight wasn't on him.

Today, Rob is a successful businessman, husband, and father living in Great Falls, Montana. His story reminds us that elite performance doesn't start with talent—it starts with mindset.

Week 1
LIVING IN THE MOMENT

"Pressure is a privilege. It only comes to those who earn it.
— Billie Jean King

Athlete Insights: From Rob Schulte

"I've learned over time to just be present and live in the moment. It's natural to feel stress or nerves, but when you accept that, it becomes easier to focus on your objective."

Rob's approach to pressure is rooted in awareness. Instead of fighting nerves or trying to be perfect, he trains himself to focus on the task in front of him. Whether it was catching a punt in a packed stadium or managing business challenges today, Rob's go-to tools are preparation, fundamentals, and being grounded in the present.

Keep that in mind as you check in this week.

Its early in the journey, sometimes that makes it hard to stay motivated or work as hard as your goals may require. That's okay, just be aware of it, and prepare in a way that allows you to overcome those traps.

Date ___/___/___

Rate each on a scale from 1-10 (1=low, 10=high)
  MOOD:___ STRESS:___ ENERGY:___ MOTIVATION:___
Am I satisfied with the work I did today to reach my goals?

☐ YES   ☐ NO

If yes, what helped today?
If no, what can I refocus on tomorrow?

Date ___/___/___

Rate each on a scale from 1-10 (1=low, 10=high)
  MOOD:___ STRESS:___ ENERGY:___ MOTIVATION:___
Am I satisfied with the work I did today to reach my goals?

☐ YES   ☐ NO

If yes, what helped today?
If no, what can I refocus on tomorrow?

Date ___/___/___

Rate each on a scale from 1-10 (1=low, 10=high)
  MOOD:___ STRESS:___ ENERGY:___ MOTIVATION:___
Am I satisfied with the work I did today to reach my goals?

☐ YES   ☐ NO

If yes, what helped today?
If no, what can I refocus on tomorrow?

Date ___/___/___

Rate each on a scale from 1-10 (1=low, 10=high)
 MOOD:___ STRESS:___ ENERGY:___ MOTIVATION:___
Am I satisfied with the work I did today to reach my goals?

☐ YES ☐ NO

If yes, what helped today?
If no, what can I refocus on tomorrow?

Date ___/___/___

Rate each on a scale from 1-10 (1=low, 10=high)
 MOOD:___ STRESS:___ ENERGY:___ MOTIVATION:___
Am I satisfied with the work I did today to reach my goals?

☐ YES ☐ NO

If yes, what helped today?
If no, what can I refocus on tomorrow?

Date ___/___/___

Rate each on a scale from 1-10 (1=low, 10=high)
 MOOD:___ STRESS:___ ENERGY:___ MOTIVATION:___
Am I satisfied with the work I did today to reach my goals?

☐ YES ☐ NO

If yes, what helped today?
If no, what can I refocus on tomorrow?

Date ___/___/___

Weekly Reflection

What emotion have I felt most often this week?

[ ]

Did I take time to notice how I was feeling before or after a big moment?

☐ YES   ☐ NO

What was the moment? What did you notice. Whether or not you forgot to pay attention to how you were feeling at the time, how do you feel about it now?

[ ]

Write about a moment that challenged you mentally this week. How did you respond?

[ ]

How intense were your practices or workouts this week? Did anything shift mentally?

[ ]

Read Aloud:

I FOCUS ON WHAT I CAN CONTROL.
I AM PREPARED AND READY.

Week 2
CONTROL THE CONTROLLABLE

> *"I can't control what everyone else does, but I can control how I prepare, how I work, and how I compete."*
>
> — Tom Brady

Athlete Insights: From Rob Schulte

"I like the acronym 'TNT'—Things that take no talent. I can focus on what I can control—having a positive attitude, setting the bar for hard work, being coachable no matter who the coach is, and focusing on my role."

Rob's philosophy is simple but powerful: not everything is within your control, but your attitude, effort, and mindset always are. He calls these "TNT" behaviors because they require zero talent but create massive impact. Especially during transitions, injuries, or tough seasons, Rob focuses on staying grounded in what he can control—his preparation, his focus, and how he supports his team.

This mindset is awareness in action. It's about tuning in to what matters and tuning out the noise.

Your job this week is to find the "TNT" areas of your life; where effort, not talent, makes the biggest impact. Good luck!

Date __/__/__

Rate each on a scale from 1-10 (1=low, 10=high)

MOOD: ___ STRESS: ___ ENERGY: ___ MOTIVATION: ___

Am I satisfied with the work I did today to reach my goals?

☐ YES ☐ NO

If yes, what helped today?
If no, what can I refocus on tomorrow?

```
[                                                    ]
```

Date __/__/__

Rate each on a scale from 1-10 (1=low, 10=high)

MOOD: ___ STRESS: ___ ENERGY: ___ MOTIVATION: ___

Am I satisfied with the work I did today to reach my goals?

☐ YES ☐ NO

If yes, what helped today?
If no, what can I refocus on tomorrow?

```
[                                                    ]
```

Date __/__/__

Rate each on a scale from 1-10 (1=low, 10=high)

MOOD: ___ STRESS: ___ ENERGY: ___ MOTIVATION: ___

Am I satisfied with the work I did today to reach my goals?

☐ YES ☐ NO

If yes, what helped today?
If no, what can I refocus on tomorrow?

```
[                                                    ]
```

Date __/__/__

Rate each on a scale from 1-10 (1=low, 10=high)

Mood: ___ Stress: ___ Energy: ___ Motivation: ___

Am I satisfied with the work I did today to reach my goals?

☐ Yes   ☐ No

If yes, what helped today?
If no, what can I refocus on tomorrow?

Date __/__/__

Rate each on a scale from 1-10 (1=low, 10=high)

Mood: ___ Stress: ___ Energy: ___ Motivation: ___

Am I satisfied with the work I did today to reach my goals?

☐ Yes   ☐ No

If yes, what helped today?
If no, what can I refocus on tomorrow?

Date __/__/__

Rate each on a scale from 1-10 (1=low, 10=high)

Mood: ___ Stress: ___ Energy: ___ Motivation: ___

Am I satisfied with the work I did today to reach my goals?

☐ Yes   ☐ No

If yes, what helped today?
If no, what can I refocus on tomorrow?

Date ___/___/___

Weekly Reflection

What emotion have I felt most often this week?

[ ]

Did I take time to notice how I was feeling before or after a big moment?

☐ YES   ☐ NO

What was the moment? What did you notice. Whether or not you forgot to pay attention to how you were feeling at the time, how do you feel about it now?

[ ]

Write about a moment that challenged you mentally this week. How did you respond?

[ ]

How intense were your practices or workouts this week? Did anything shift mentally?

[ ]

Read Aloud:

**I FOCUS ON WHAT I CAN CONTROL.
I AM PREPARED AND READY.**

Week 3
REFLECT TO IMPROVE

"Success comes from knowing that you did your best to become the best that you are capable of becoming"

— John Wooden

Athlete Insights: From Rob Schulte

"You either get better or you get worse. There is no such thing as staying the same. The best athletes are always looking at the next detail to get better."

Rob does not believe in neutral ground. His awareness is rooted in constant self-checks—small questions, honest answers, and the willingness to learn. Whether he was preparing for a game, recovering from a setback, or helping his team from the sidelines, Rob always used reflection as a tool to grow.

This week, we challenge you to take an honest look at your habits, your progress, and your role. Reflection is not about perfection. It is about being aware of where you are and what needs your attention next.

Date __/__/__

Rate each on a scale from 1-10 (1=low, 10=high)
  MOOD: ___   STRESS: ___   ENERGY: ___   MOTIVATION: ___
Am I satisfied with the work I did today to reach my goals?

☐ YES   ☐ NO

If yes, what helped today?
If no, what can I refocus on tomorrow?

Date __/__/__

Rate each on a scale from 1-10 (1=low, 10=high)
  MOOD: ___   STRESS: ___   ENERGY: ___   MOTIVATION: ___
Am I satisfied with the work I did today to reach my goals?

☐ YES   ☐ NO

If yes, what helped today?
If no, what can I refocus on tomorrow?

Date __/__/__

Rate each on a scale from 1-10 (1=low, 10=high)
  MOOD: ___   STRESS: ___   ENERGY: ___   MOTIVATION: ___
Am I satisfied with the work I did today to reach my goals?

☐ YES   ☐ NO

If yes, what helped today?
If no, what can I refocus on tomorrow?

Date ___/___/___

Rate each on a scale from 1-10 (1=low, 10=high)
  MOOD:___ STRESS:___ ENERGY:___ MOTIVATION:___

Am I satisfied with the work I did today to reach my goals?

☐ YES   ☐ NO

If yes, what helped today?
If no, what can I refocus on tomorrow?

Date ___/___/___

Rate each on a scale from 1-10 (1=low, 10=high)
  MOOD:___ STRESS:___ ENERGY:___ MOTIVATION:___

Am I satisfied with the work I did today to reach my goals?

☐ YES   ☐ NO

If yes, what helped today?
If no, what can I refocus on tomorrow?

Date ___/___/___

Rate each on a scale from 1-10 (1=low, 10=high)
  MOOD:___ STRESS:___ ENERGY:___ MOTIVATION:___

Am I satisfied with the work I did today to reach my goals?

☐ YES   ☐ NO

If yes, what helped today?
If no, what can I refocus on tomorrow?

Date ___/___/___

Weekly Reflection

What emotion have I felt most often this week?

[ ]

Did I take time to notice how I was feeling before or after a big moment?

☐ YES   ☐ NO

What was the moment? What did you notice. Whether or not you forgot to pay attention to how you were feeling at the time, how do you feel about it now?

[ ]

Write about a moment that challenged you mentally this week. How did you respond?

[ ]

How intense were your practices or workouts this week? Did anything shift mentally?

[ ]

Read Aloud:

I FOCUS ON WHAT I CAN CONTROL.
I AM PREPARED AND READY.

Week 4
OWN YOUR ROLE

"Do your job."

— Bill Belichick

Athlete Insights: From Rob Schulte

"One of my biggest accomplishments in college was being named Scout Team Player of the Year. I got my butt whipped for 16 weeks straight, but my goal was always to make the team better."

During his redshirt year at the University of Montana, Rob was not a starter. He was not even on the field during games. But instead of checking out or complaining, he leaned in. He treated every practice like his Super Bowl and every rep like it mattered. That season, the Grizzlies made it to the National Championship—and Rob believed his behind-the-scenes role made a difference.

Being aware of your role, and giving everything you have to it, is a sign of strength. Whether you're starting or sitting, leading or learning, your presence matters. And when you do your part with intention and effort, the whole team wins.

Date ___/___/___

Rate each on a scale from 1-10 (1=low, 10=high)
 MOOD:___ STRESS:___ ENERGY:___ MOTIVATION:___

Am I satisfied with the work I did today to reach my goals?

☐ YES ☐ NO

If yes, what helped today?
If no, what can I refocus on tomorrow?

Date ___/___/___

Rate each on a scale from 1-10 (1=low, 10=high)
 MOOD:___ STRESS:___ ENERGY:___ MOTIVATION:___

Am I satisfied with the work I did today to reach my goals?

☐ YES ☐ NO

If yes, what helped today?
If no, what can I refocus on tomorrow?

Date ___/___/___

Rate each on a scale from 1-10 (1=low, 10=high)
 MOOD:___ STRESS:___ ENERGY:___ MOTIVATION:___

Am I satisfied with the work I did today to reach my goals?

☐ YES ☐ NO

If yes, what helped today?
If no, what can I refocus on tomorrow?

Date __/__/__

Rate each on a scale from 1-10 (1=low, 10=high)

Mood: ___ Stress: ___ Energy: ___ Motivation: ___

Am I satisfied with the work I did today to reach my goals?

☐ Yes ☐ No

If yes, what helped today?
If no, what can I refocus on tomorrow?

Date __/__/__

Rate each on a scale from 1-10 (1=low, 10=high)

Mood: ___ Stress: ___ Energy: ___ Motivation: ___

Am I satisfied with the work I did today to reach my goals?

☐ Yes ☐ No

If yes, what helped today?
If no, what can I refocus on tomorrow?

Date __/__/__

Rate each on a scale from 1-10 (1=low, 10=high)

Mood: ___ Stress: ___ Energy: ___ Motivation: ___

Am I satisfied with the work I did today to reach my goals?

☐ Yes ☐ No

If yes, what helped today?
If no, what can I refocus on tomorrow?

Date ___/___/___

Weekly Reflection

What emotion have I felt most often this week?

[   ]

Did I take time to notice how I was feeling before or after a big moment?

☐ YES ☐ NO

What was the moment? What did you notice. Whether or not you forgot to pay attention to how you were feeling at the time, how do you feel about it now?

[   ]

Write about a moment that challenged you mentally this week. How did you respond?

[   ]

How intense were your practices or workouts this week? Did anything shift mentally?

[   ]

Read Aloud:

I FOCUS ON WHAT I CAN CONTROL.
I AM PREPARED AND READY.

MONTH 2
Focus

What is Focus?

Focus is the ability to block out distractions, pressure, and noise—and lock in on the task in front of you. In sports, it means tuning in to your role, the next play, or the feeling of your body during a rep. Focus can be physical, mental, or emotional. It sharpens your performance and gives you the power to bounce back quickly when something doesn't go your way.

Athletes who build strong focus routines train their attention the same way they train their bodies. They learn how to stay present under pressure, how to reset between plays, and how to get the most out of their preparation.

This month, you'll hear from Aaron DeFrance, a multi-sport athlete who has learned how to trust his preparation, stay composed under pressure, and push forward when it matters most.

Meet the Athlete:

Aaron DeFrance

Aaron DeFrance is a three-sport athlete from Montana, excelling in basketball, baseball, and golf. After transferring from Harrison to finish his senior year at Three Forks High School, Aaron helped lead the Wolves to district and postseason basketball titles and a third-place finish at the State Tournament. He also played a key role in securing a trophy for the Wolves at the State Golf Tournament.

Now playing college basketball at Dawson Community College, Aaron continues to chase the goals he's been dreaming about his whole life. He brings calm intensity, discipline, and a quiet kind of focus to everything he does.

"It's been a dream my whole life to play college basketball, and now that it is coming together, I'm super excited and I cannot wait."

Week 5
TRUSTING THE WORK

"The more you sweat in practice, the less you bleed in battle."
- *Navy SEAL Motto*

Athlete Insights: From Aaron DeFrance

"I handle pressure and stress by breathing and trusting myself with the work that I have put in to be successful."

Aaron's focus is built on preparation. Instead of overthinking, he centers himself with breathing, self-trust, and confidence in his training. He knows that if the work is there, the results will come. That kind of trust creates a powerful internal calm.

Focus is not about being perfect. It is about being present. And that starts with trusting your process.

Date ___/___/___

Rate each on a scale from 1-10 (1=low, 10=high)
 MOOD:___ STRESS:___ ENERGY:___ MOTIVATION:___
Am I satisfied with the work I did today to reach my goals?

☐ YES ☐ NO

If yes, what helped today?
If no, what can I refocus on tomorrow?

Date ___/___/___

Rate each on a scale from 1-10 (1=low, 10=high)
 MOOD:___ STRESS:___ ENERGY:___ MOTIVATION:___
Am I satisfied with the work I did today to reach my goals?

☐ YES ☐ NO

If yes, what helped today?
If no, what can I refocus on tomorrow?

Date ___/___/___

Rate each on a scale from 1-10 (1=low, 10=high)
 MOOD:___ STRESS:___ ENERGY:___ MOTIVATION:___
Am I satisfied with the work I did today to reach my goals?

☐ YES ☐ NO

If yes, what helped today?
If no, what can I refocus on tomorrow?

Date ___/___/___

Rate each on a scale from 1-10 (1=low, 10=high)
 MOOD:___ STRESS:___ ENERGY:___ MOTIVATION:___

Am I satisfied with the work I did today to reach my goals?

☐ YES ☐ NO

If yes, what helped today?
If no, what can I refocus on tomorrow?

Date ___/___/___

Rate each on a scale from 1-10 (1=low, 10=high)
 MOOD:___ STRESS:___ ENERGY:___ MOTIVATION:___

Am I satisfied with the work I did today to reach my goals?

☐ YES ☐ NO

If yes, what helped today?
If no, what can I refocus on tomorrow?

Date ___/___/___

Rate each on a scale from 1-10 (1=low, 10=high)
 MOOD:___ STRESS:___ ENERGY:___ MOTIVATION:___

Am I satisfied with the work I did today to reach my goals?

☐ YES ☐ NO

If yes, what helped today?
If no, what can I refocus on tomorrow?

Date ___/___/___

Weekly Reflection

What emotion have I felt most often this week?

[ ]

Did I take time to notice how I was feeling before or after a big moment?

☐ YES   ☐ NO

What was the moment? What did you notice. Whether or not you forgot to pay attention to how you were feeling at the time, how do you feel about it now?

[ ]

Write about a moment that challenged you mentally this week. How did you respond?

[ ]

How intense were your practices or workouts this week? Did anything shift mentally?

[ ]

Read Aloud:
> **I FOCUS ON WHAT I CAN CONTROL.**
> **I AM PREPARED AND READY.**

Week 6
SHORT-TERM MEMORY

"You can't let one mistake turn into two.."

- Nick Saban

Athlete Insights: From Aaron DeFrance

"To handle setbacks, I try to forget and have short-term memory while also learning from mistakes and working hard to improve."

This week, we're focusing on one of the most valuable tools in any athlete's mental toolbox: short-term memory. That means letting go of the last play—good or bad—and locking into the next one. Aaron understands that the only way to grow is to learn from mistakes without getting stuck in them.

Focus is not just about paying attention. It's also about releasing distractions. When you carry frustration or self-doubt from one moment to the next, it takes up space in your mind that should be used for performance. The best players reset fast and refocus faster.

Mistakes are part of the game. What matters most is what you do next.

Date ___/___/___

Rate each on a scale from 1-10 (1=low, 10=high)
 MOOD: ___ STRESS: ___ ENERGY: ___ MOTIVATION: ___
Am I satisfied with the work I did today to reach my goals?

☐ YES   ☐ NO

If yes, what helped today?
If no, what can I refocus on tomorrow?

Date ___/___/___

Rate each on a scale from 1-10 (1=low, 10=high)
 MOOD: ___ STRESS: ___ ENERGY: ___ MOTIVATION: ___
Am I satisfied with the work I did today to reach my goals?

☐ YES   ☐ NO

If yes, what helped today?
If no, what can I refocus on tomorrow?

Date ___/___/___

Rate each on a scale from 1-10 (1=low, 10=high)
 MOOD: ___ STRESS: ___ ENERGY: ___ MOTIVATION: ___
Am I satisfied with the work I did today to reach my goals?

☐ YES   ☐ NO

If yes, what helped today?
If no, what can I refocus on tomorrow?

Date ___/___/___

Rate each on a scale from 1-10 (1=low, 10=high)

MOOD:___ STRESS:___ ENERGY:___ MOTIVATION:___

Am I satisfied with the work I did today to reach my goals?

☐ YES   ☐ NO

If yes, what helped today?
If no, what can I refocus on tomorrow?

Date ___/___/___

Rate each on a scale from 1-10 (1=low, 10=high)

MOOD:___ STRESS:___ ENERGY:___ MOTIVATION:___

Am I satisfied with the work I did today to reach my goals?

☐ YES   ☐ NO

If yes, what helped today?
If no, what can I refocus on tomorrow?

Date ___/___/___

Rate each on a scale from 1-10 (1=low, 10=high)

MOOD:___ STRESS:___ ENERGY:___ MOTIVATION:___

Am I satisfied with the work I did today to reach my goals?

☐ YES   ☐ NO

If yes, what helped today?
If no, what can I refocus on tomorrow?

Date ___/___/___

Weekly Reflection

What emotion have I felt most often this week?

[   ]

Did I take time to notice how I was feeling before or after a big moment?

☐ YES   ☐ NO

What was the moment? What did you notice. Whether or not you forgot to pay attention to how you were feeling at the time, how do you feel about it now?

[   ]

Write about a moment that challenged you mentally this week. How did you respond?

[   ]

How intense were your practices or workouts this week? Did anything shift mentally?

[   ]

Read Aloud:

I FOCUS ON WHAT I CAN CONTROL.
I AM PREPARED AND READY.

Week 7
BLOCK OUT THE NOISE

"If you listen to the crowd, you'll never lead the orchestra.."

- Unknown

Athlete Insights: From Aaron DeFrance

"I trust myself and the work that I have put in that I can have success without negativity coming from the outside and not listening to negative comments."

Focus is not just about where you look—it's about what you ignore. Aaron stays locked in by trusting his preparation and blocking out external noise. Whether it's criticism, comparison, or pressure from others, he tunes it out and turns inward. His focus comes from confidence in the work.

This week is about building your own internal focus. That means listening to your goals, your coaches, and your inner drive—not random voices on the sidelines.

You do not need everyone's approval to stay on your path. Focus is often quiet.

Date ___ / ___ / ___

Rate each on a scale from 1-10 (1=low, 10=high)
MOOD: ___ STRESS: ___ ENERGY: ___ MOTIVATION: ___

Am I satisfied with the work I did today to reach my goals?

☐ YES   ☐ NO

If yes, what helped today?
If no, what can I refocus on tomorrow?

Date ___ / ___ / ___

Rate each on a scale from 1-10 (1=low, 10=high)
MOOD: ___ STRESS: ___ ENERGY: ___ MOTIVATION: ___

Am I satisfied with the work I did today to reach my goals?

☐ YES   ☐ NO

If yes, what helped today?
If no, what can I refocus on tomorrow?

Date ___ / ___ / ___

Rate each on a scale from 1-10 (1=low, 10=high)
MOOD: ___ STRESS: ___ ENERGY: ___ MOTIVATION: ___

Am I satisfied with the work I did today to reach my goals?

☐ YES   ☐ NO

If yes, what helped today?
If no, what can I refocus on tomorrow?

Date ___/___/___

Rate each on a scale from 1-10 (1=low, 10=high)
 MOOD:___ STRESS:___ ENERGY:___ MOTIVATION:___

Am I satisfied with the work I did today to reach my goals?

☐ YES ☐ NO

If yes, what helped today?
If no, what can I refocus on tomorrow?

Date ___/___/___

Rate each on a scale from 1-10 (1=low, 10=high)
 MOOD:___ STRESS:___ ENERGY:___ MOTIVATION:___

Am I satisfied with the work I did today to reach my goals?

☐ YES ☐ NO

If yes, what helped today?
If no, what can I refocus on tomorrow?

Date ___/___/___

Rate each on a scale from 1-10 (1=low, 10=high)
 MOOD:___ STRESS:___ ENERGY:___ MOTIVATION:___

Am I satisfied with the work I did today to reach my goals?

☐ YES ☐ NO

If yes, what helped today?
If no, what can I refocus on tomorrow?

Date ___/___/___

Weekly Reflection

What emotion have I felt most often this week?

```
[                                                    ]
```

Did I take time to notice how I was feeling before or after a big moment?

☐ YES   ☐ NO

What was the moment? What did you notice. Whether or not you forgot to pay attention to how you were feeling at the time, how do you feel about it now?

```
[                                                    ]
```

Write about a moment that challenged you mentally this week. How did you respond?

```
[                                                    ]
```

How intense were your practices or workouts this week? Did anything shift mentally?

```
[                                                    ]
```

Read Aloud:

**I FOCUS ON WHAT I CAN CONTROL.
I AM PREPARED AND READY.**

Week 8
FOCUS UNDER PRESSURE

"Pressure is something you feel when you don't know what you're doing."

- Chuck Noll

Athlete Insights: From Aaron DeFrance

"I sometimes try to think about something else and breathe through the nerves, but in most cases I have to use the nerves to my advantage. Once something good happens in a game, the nerves go away and I can play free—which is when I'm at my best."

Pressure is part of the game. Some athletes panic when it shows up. Others learn to use it. Aaron leans into the nerves, knowing that energy is fuel. His secret? Preparation and self-awareness. He takes a breath, trusts the work, and uses early momentum to unlock freedom and flow.

This week's focus is all about performing when it counts. Whether it's a big game, an important practice, or a tough conversation—pressure is an opportunity, not an enemy.

Preparation builds confidence. Awareness keeps it steady.

Date __/__/__

Rate each on a scale from 1-10 (1=low, 10=high)
 MOOD:___ STRESS:___ ENERGY:___ MOTIVATION:___

Am I satisfied with the work I did today to reach my goals?

☐ YES ☐ NO

If yes, what helped today?
If no, what can I refocus on tomorrow?

Date __/__/__

Rate each on a scale from 1-10 (1=low, 10=high)
 MOOD:___ STRESS:___ ENERGY:___ MOTIVATION:___

Am I satisfied with the work I did today to reach my goals?

☐ YES ☐ NO

If yes, what helped today?
If no, what can I refocus on tomorrow?

Date __/__/__

Rate each on a scale from 1-10 (1=low, 10=high)
 MOOD:___ STRESS:___ ENERGY:___ MOTIVATION:___

Am I satisfied with the work I did today to reach my goals?

☐ YES ☐ NO

If yes, what helped today?
If no, what can I refocus on tomorrow?

Date ___/___/___

Rate each on a scale from 1-10 (1=low, 10=high)

MOOD:___ STRESS:___ ENERGY:___ MOTIVATION:___

Am I satisfied with the work I did today to reach my goals?

☐ YES ☐ NO

If yes, what helped today?
If no, what can I refocus on tomorrow?

Date ___/___/___

Rate each on a scale from 1-10 (1=low, 10=high)

MOOD:___ STRESS:___ ENERGY:___ MOTIVATION:___

Am I satisfied with the work I did today to reach my goals?

☐ YES ☐ NO

If yes, what helped today?
If no, what can I refocus on tomorrow?

Date ___/___/___

Rate each on a scale from 1-10 (1=low, 10=high)

MOOD:___ STRESS:___ ENERGY:___ MOTIVATION:___

Am I satisfied with the work I did today to reach my goals?

☐ YES ☐ NO

If yes, what helped today?
If no, what can I refocus on tomorrow?

Date ___/___/___

Weekly Reflection

What emotion have I felt most often this week?

[   ]

Did I take time to notice how I was feeling before or after a big moment?

☐ YES   ☐ NO

What was the moment? What did you notice. Whether or not you forgot to pay attention to how you were feeling at the time, how do you feel about it now?

[   ]

Write about a moment that challenged you mentally this week. How did you respond?

[   ]

How intense were your practices or workouts this week? Did anything shift mentally?

[   ]

Read Aloud:
> **I FOCUS ON WHAT I CAN CONTROL.**
> **I AM PREPARED AND READY.**

MONTH 3
Resilience

What is Resilience?

Resilience is the ability to continue forward when things do not go as planned. It is not the absence of struggle, stress, or failure. It is the willingness to stay committed through them. Resilience is built when you face pressure without panic, setbacks without losing direction, and uncertainty without giving up your purpose.

For athletes, resilience shows up in preparation, perspective, and persistence. It means breaking big moments into manageable steps. It means learning from loss without letting it define you. It means continuing to work, even when the path forward looks different than expected.

This month, you will learn from Aleksei Grosulak, whose journey reflects toughness, faith, and steady commitment through challenge and change.

Meet the Athlete:
Aleksei Grosulak

Aleksei Grosulak was born and raised in Billings, Montana, where he built a standout high school career at Billings Central. He helped lead the Rams to two straight Class A state championship game appearances, earning all-state honors twice and Great Falls Tribune Super-State recognition as a senior. Aleksei was also a key contributor to the Billings Scarlets American Legion baseball program, earning all-state honors on a back-to-back state championship team.

He went on to compete at Montana State University, where he was named co-winner of the Chuck Karnop Toughness Award following spring drills, an honor that reflects grit, work ethic, and resilience. After graduating, Aleksei spent five years working in chemical engineering while moving across four different states, continuing to apply the same mental toughness beyond athletics.

Week 9
TRUE TEST OF STRENGTH

"One step at a time is still progress."
— Unknown

Athlete Insights: From Aleksei Grosulak

"I lean on knowing the hours of preparation I put into my craft and break the moment into steps so it does not get too big."

Resilience often begins with simplification. Aleksei does not allow pressure to overwhelm him. When the moment feels heavy, he narrows his focus to what comes next. This approach keeps emotions from spiraling and allows preparation to take over.

This week is about managing pressure by staying present. You do not need to solve everything at once. You only need to handle the next step.

Focus on the next step, don't get lost in the past or too far in the future.

Date ___/___/___

Rate each on a scale from 1-10 (1=low, 10=high)
 MOOD:___ STRESS:___ ENERGY:___ MOTIVATION:___
Am I satisfied with the work I did today to reach my goals?

☐ YES ☐ NO

If yes, what helped today?
If no, what can I refocus on tomorrow?

Date ___/___/___

Rate each on a scale from 1-10 (1=low, 10=high)
 MOOD:___ STRESS:___ ENERGY:___ MOTIVATION:___
Am I satisfied with the work I did today to reach my goals?

☐ YES ☐ NO

If yes, what helped today?
If no, what can I refocus on tomorrow?

Date ___/___/___

Rate each on a scale from 1-10 (1=low, 10=high)
 MOOD:___ STRESS:___ ENERGY:___ MOTIVATION:___
Am I satisfied with the work I did today to reach my goals?

☐ YES ☐ NO

If yes, what helped today?
If no, what can I refocus on tomorrow?

Date ___/___/___

Rate each on a scale from 1-10 (1=low, 10=high)
MOOD:___ STRESS:___ ENERGY:___ MOTIVATION:___

Am I satisfied with the work I did today to reach my goals?

☐ YES   ☐ NO

If yes, what helped today?
If no, what can I refocus on tomorrow?

Date ___/___/___

Rate each on a scale from 1-10 (1=low, 10=high)
MOOD:___ STRESS:___ ENERGY:___ MOTIVATION:___

Am I satisfied with the work I did today to reach my goals?

☐ YES   ☐ NO

If yes, what helped today?
If no, what can I refocus on tomorrow?

Date ___/___/___

Rate each on a scale from 1-10 (1=low, 10=high)
MOOD:___ STRESS:___ ENERGY:___ MOTIVATION:___

Am I satisfied with the work I did today to reach my goals?

☐ YES   ☐ NO

If yes, what helped today?
If no, what can I refocus on tomorrow?

Date ___ / ___ / ___

Weekly Reflection

What emotion have I felt most often this week?

Did I take time to notice how I was feeling before or after a big moment?

☐ YES   ☐ NO

What was the moment? What did you notice. Whether or not you forgot to pay attention to how you were feeling at the time, how do you feel about it now?

Write about a moment that challenged you mentally this week. How did you respond?

How intense were your practices or workouts this week? Did anything shift mentally?

Read Aloud:

I FOCUS ON WHAT I CAN CONTROL.
I AM PREPARED AND READY.

Week 10
ACCEPTING SETBACKS

"Failure is simply the opportunity to begin again, this time more intelligently."
- Henry Ford

Athlete Insights: From Aleksei Grosulak

"A setback does not change the goal. It provides a new path to accomplish it."

Resilient athletes do not see setbacks as endings. Aleksei understands that adversity often forces adjustment, not abandonment. When things go wrong, he stays positive and searches for a new approach rather than losing sight of the destination.

This week is about reframing difficulty. The goal remains the same. The route may change.

Remind yourself to stay committed to the goal while remaining flexible in the path.

Date __/__/__

Rate each on a scale from 1-10 (1=low, 10=high)
MOOD:___ STRESS:___ ENERGY:___ MOTIVATION:___

Am I satisfied with the work I did today to reach my goals?

☐ YES　　　☐ NO

If yes, what helped today?
If no, what can I refocus on tomorrow?

Date __/__/__

Rate each on a scale from 1-10 (1=low, 10=high)
MOOD:___ STRESS:___ ENERGY:___ MOTIVATION:___

Am I satisfied with the work I did today to reach my goals?

☐ YES　　　☐ NO

If yes, what helped today?
If no, what can I refocus on tomorrow?

Date __/__/__

Rate each on a scale from 1-10 (1=low, 10=high)
MOOD:___ STRESS:___ ENERGY:___ MOTIVATION:___

Am I satisfied with the work I did today to reach my goals?

☐ YES　　　☐ NO

If yes, what helped today?
If no, what can I refocus on tomorrow?

Date ___/___/___

Rate each on a scale from 1-10 (1=low, 10=high)

MOOD: ___ STRESS: ___ ENERGY: ___ MOTIVATION: ___

Am I satisfied with the work I did today to reach my goals?

☐ YES ☐ NO

If yes, what helped today?
If no, what can I refocus on tomorrow?

Date ___/___/___

Rate each on a scale from 1-10 (1=low, 10=high)

MOOD: ___ STRESS: ___ ENERGY: ___ MOTIVATION: ___

Am I satisfied with the work I did today to reach my goals?

☐ YES ☐ NO

If yes, what helped today?
If no, what can I refocus on tomorrow?

Date ___/___/___

Rate each on a scale from 1-10 (1=low, 10=high)

MOOD: ___ STRESS: ___ ENERGY: ___ MOTIVATION: ___

Am I satisfied with the work I did today to reach my goals?

☐ YES ☐ NO

If yes, what helped today?
If no, what can I refocus on tomorrow?

Date ___/___/___

Weekly Reflection

What emotion have I felt most often this week?

```
[                                                    ]
```

Did I take time to notice how I was feeling before or after a big moment?

☐ YES   ☐ NO

What was the moment? What did you notice. Whether or not you forgot to pay attention to how you were feeling at the time, how do you feel about it now?

```
[                                                    ]
```

Write about a moment that challenged you mentally this week. How did you respond?

```
[                                                    ]
```

How intense were your practices or workouts this week? Did anything shift mentally?

```
[                                                    ]
```

Read Aloud:

**I FOCUS ON WHAT I CAN CONTROL.
I AM PREPARED AND READY.**

BE COACHABLE

"If you want to go fast, go alone. If you want to go far, go together."
- African Proverb

Athlete Insights: From Aleksei Grosulak

"Do not take criticism personally. Use it as an opportunity to improve. If they are not telling you anything, then they do not care about you."

Being coachable is a core part of resilience. Aleksei understands that feedback is not about tearing you down. It is about helping you improve. Coaches invest time and energy into athletes they believe in. Silence is not comfort. Silence is distance.

This week is about separating emotion from instruction. When you stay open to coaching, you give yourself the chance to grow faster and more intentionally. Resilient athletes listen, adjust, and respond with effort.

Stay humble and hungry to learn. Growth begins with coachability.

Date ___/___/___

Rate each on a scale from 1-10 (1=low, 10=high)
 MOOD: ___ STRESS: ___ ENERGY: ___ MOTIVATION: ___

Am I satisfied with the work I did today to reach my goals?

☐ YES ☐ NO

If yes, what helped today?
If no, what can I refocus on tomorrow?

Date ___/___/___

Rate each on a scale from 1-10 (1=low, 10=high)
 MOOD: ___ STRESS: ___ ENERGY: ___ MOTIVATION: ___

Am I satisfied with the work I did today to reach my goals?

☐ YES ☐ NO

If yes, what helped today?
If no, what can I refocus on tomorrow?

Date ___/___/___

Rate each on a scale from 1-10 (1=low, 10=high)
 MOOD: ___ STRESS: ___ ENERGY: ___ MOTIVATION: ___

Am I satisfied with the work I did today to reach my goals?

☐ YES ☐ NO

If yes, what helped today?
If no, what can I refocus on tomorrow?

Date ___/___/___

Rate each on a scale from 1-10 (1=low, 10=high)
  MOOD:___ STRESS:___ ENERGY:___ MOTIVATION:___

Am I satisfied with the work I did today to reach my goals?

☐ YES ☐ NO

If yes, what helped today?
If no, what can I refocus on tomorrow?

Date ___/___/___

Rate each on a scale from 1-10 (1=low, 10=high)
  MOOD:___ STRESS:___ ENERGY:___ MOTIVATION:___

Am I satisfied with the work I did today to reach my goals?

☐ YES ☐ NO

If yes, what helped today?
If no, what can I refocus on tomorrow?

Date ___/___/___

Rate each on a scale from 1-10 (1=low, 10=high)
  MOOD:___ STRESS:___ ENERGY:___ MOTIVATION:___

Am I satisfied with the work I did today to reach my goals?

☐ YES ☐ NO

If yes, what helped today?
If no, what can I refocus on tomorrow?

Date __/__/__

Weekly Reflection

What emotion have I felt most often this week?

```
[                                                    ]
```

Did I take time to notice how I was feeling before or after a big moment?

☐ YES　　　☐ No

What was the moment? What did you notice. Whether or not you forgot to pay attention to how you were feeling at the time, how do you feel about it now?

```
[                                                    ]
```

Write about a moment that challenged you mentally this week. How did you respond?

```
[                                                    ]
```

How intense were your practices or workouts this week? Did anything shift mentally?

```
[                                                    ]
```

Read Aloud:

I FOCUS ON WHAT I CAN CONTROL.
I AM PREPARED AND READY.

PERSPECTIVE

"Hardships often prepare ordinary people for an extraordinary destiny."
— C.S. Lewis

Athlete Insights: From Aleksei Grosulak

"I know I will not be given a cross I cannot carry."

Alexi's mindset around recovery has shifted with experience. He no longer sees rest as weakness. Instead, he views it as a skill. Building strength, stamina, and resilience means allowing your body and brain time to recharge. That includes sleep, nutrition, physical rest, and even mental space away from the sport.

This week is about developing habits of rest and recovery. Resilience is not just about grinding. It is also about learning when to pause, reflect, and come back stronger.

Recovery is not a break from resilience. It is a part of it.

Date ___/___/___

Rate each on a scale from 1-10 (1=low, 10=high)

MOOD:___ STRESS:___ ENERGY:___ MOTIVATION:___

Am I satisfied with the work I did today to reach my goals?

☐ YES ☐ NO

If yes, what helped today?
If no, what can I refocus on tomorrow?

Date ___/___/___

Rate each on a scale from 1-10 (1=low, 10=high)

MOOD:___ STRESS:___ ENERGY:___ MOTIVATION:___

Am I satisfied with the work I did today to reach my goals?

☐ YES ☐ NO

If yes, what helped today?
If no, what can I refocus on tomorrow?

Date ___/___/___

Rate each on a scale from 1-10 (1=low, 10=high)

MOOD:___ STRESS:___ ENERGY:___ MOTIVATION:___

Am I satisfied with the work I did today to reach my goals?

☐ YES ☐ NO

If yes, what helped today?
If no, what can I refocus on tomorrow?

Date ___/___/___

Rate each on a scale from 1-10 (1=low, 10=high)

MOOD: ___ STRESS: ___ ENERGY: ___ MOTIVATION: ___

Am I satisfied with the work I did today to reach my goals?

☐ YES ☐ NO

If yes, what helped today?
If no, what can I refocus on tomorrow?

Date ___/___/___

Rate each on a scale from 1-10 (1=low, 10=high)

MOOD: ___ STRESS: ___ ENERGY: ___ MOTIVATION: ___

Am I satisfied with the work I did today to reach my goals?

☐ YES ☐ NO

If yes, what helped today?
If no, what can I refocus on tomorrow?

Date ___/___/___

Rate each on a scale from 1-10 (1=low, 10=high)

MOOD: ___ STRESS: ___ ENERGY: ___ MOTIVATION: ___

Am I satisfied with the work I did today to reach my goals?

☐ YES ☐ NO

If yes, what helped today?
If no, what can I refocus on tomorrow?

Date ___/___/___

Weekly Reflection

What emotion have I felt most often this week?

[   ]

Did I take time to notice how I was feeling before or after a big moment?

☐ YES   ☐ NO

What was the moment? What did you notice. Whether or not you forgot to pay attention to how you were feeling at the time, how do you feel about it now?

[   ]

Write about a moment that challenged you mentally this week. How did you respond?

[   ]

How intense were your practices or workouts this week? Did anything shift mentally?

[   ]

Read Aloud:

I FOCUS ON WHAT I CAN CONTROL.
I AM PREPARED AND READY.

MONTH 4
Confidence

What is Confidence?

Confidence is not loud. It is not flashy. Real confidence comes from knowing who you are, trusting your preparation, and believing you have value—no matter the outcome. Confidence shows up in the quiet moments when you reset after failure, the bold ones when you take the shot, and the honest ones when you ask for help.

In sports, confidence is often misunderstood as ego. But the best athletes know confidence is built from humility, repetition, reflection, and resilience.

This month, you'll learn from Blair Stapleton, an All-American Honorable Mention, team captain, and Academic All-Conference standout. Her story is one of internal growth, learning to accept criticism, lead teammates through difficult times, and ask for help when it mattered most.

Meet the Athlete:
> *Blair Stapleton*

Blair Stapleton played forward for the Carroll College Saints from 2019–2022, where she was named an All-American Honorable Mention, Scholar All-American, and team captain during her senior season. She ranks among the top 15 all-time goal scorers in program history and earned back-to-back Cascade Conference Honorable Mentions while balancing a 4.0 GPA and being named Most Inspirational Player by her teammates.

Before college, Blair starred for Billings Senior High, earning all-state honors, three MVPs, and double-digit goals across her junior and senior seasons.

Today, Blair works as the Public Outreach Coordinator for the Commissioner of Securities and Insurance. Her commitment to leadership and advocacy continues far beyond the pitch.

Week 13
CONFIDENCE THROUGH ACCEPTANCE

"Confidence comes not from always being right but from not fearing to be wrong"
— *Peter T. McIntyre*

Athlete Insights: From Blair Stapleton

"I've learned to accept criticism very well because it means someone cares. It's meaningful when someone gives you feedback—they care enough to want you to improve."

Confidence does not mean pretending you have it all figured out. Blair learned that real confidence is built by being coachable. When someone takes the time to push you, it means they believe in your potential. The key is learning how to accept feedback with clarity—not defensiveness—and use it to improve.

This week is about building confidence from the inside out. Accept feedback. Own your growth. Let the process build you.

Confidence is built by staying open to growth and not afraid of feedback.

Date ___/___/___

Rate each on a scale from 1-10 (1=low, 10=high)
 MOOD:___ STRESS:___ ENERGY:___ MOTIVATION:___

Am I satisfied with the work I did today to reach my goals?

☐ YES ☐ NO

If yes, what helped today?
If no, what can I refocus on tomorrow?

Date ___/___/___

Rate each on a scale from 1-10 (1=low, 10=high)
 MOOD:___ STRESS:___ ENERGY:___ MOTIVATION:___

Am I satisfied with the work I did today to reach my goals?

☐ YES ☐ NO

If yes, what helped today?
If no, what can I refocus on tomorrow?

Date ___/___/___

Rate each on a scale from 1-10 (1=low, 10=high)
 MOOD:___ STRESS:___ ENERGY:___ MOTIVATION:___

Am I satisfied with the work I did today to reach my goals?

☐ YES ☐ NO

If yes, what helped today?
If no, what can I refocus on tomorrow?

Date ___/___/___

Rate each on a scale from 1-10 (1=low, 10=high)
  MOOD:___ STRESS:___ ENERGY:___ MOTIVATION:___

Am I satisfied with the work I did today to reach my goals?

☐ YES   ☐ NO

If yes, what helped today?
If no, what can I refocus on tomorrow?

Date ___/___/___

Rate each on a scale from 1-10 (1=low, 10=high)
  MOOD:___ STRESS:___ ENERGY:___ MOTIVATION:___

Am I satisfied with the work I did today to reach my goals?

☐ YES   ☐ NO

If yes, what helped today?
If no, what can I refocus on tomorrow?

Date ___/___/___

Rate each on a scale from 1-10 (1=low, 10=high)
  MOOD:___ STRESS:___ ENERGY:___ MOTIVATION:___

Am I satisfied with the work I did today to reach my goals?

☐ YES   ☐ NO

If yes, what helped today?
If no, what can I refocus on tomorrow?

Date ___/___/___

Weekly Reflection

What emotion have I felt most often this week?

[ ]

Did I take time to notice how I was feeling before or after a big moment?

☐ YES   ☐ NO

What was the moment? What did you notice. Whether or not you forgot to pay attention to how you were feeling at the time, how do you feel about it now?

[ ]

Write about a moment that challenged you mentally this week. How did you respond?

[ ]

How intense were your practices or workouts this week? Did anything shift mentally?

[ ]

Read Aloud:

I FOCUS ON WHAT I CAN CONTROL.
I AM PREPARED AND READY.

Week 14
FEEL IT, THEN FREE IT

"Confidence is not 'they will like me.' Confidence is 'I'll be okay if they don't.'"
- *Christina Grimmie*

Athlete Insights: From Blair Stapleton

"After losing a game, you have one hour to be upset, angry, sad, etc. You can feel all those emotions for one hour. Then, after 60 minutes, you let it go."

Confidence is not about avoiding disappointment—it's about learning how to manage it. Blair developed a powerful emotional reset tool: give yourself space to feel, but not forever. After a loss, she lets the emotions come—but sets a clear boundary. When the clock hits 60 minutes, she lets it go and gets back to work.

This week is about regulating your emotions in a healthy way. Feel what you feel, but don't stay stuck there.

Confidence means honoring your emotions without letting them control you.

Date __/__/__

Rate each on a scale from 1-10 (1=low, 10=high)
 MOOD:___ STRESS:___ ENERGY:___ MOTIVATION:___
Am I satisfied with the work I did today to reach my goals?

☐ YES   ☐ NO

If yes, what helped today?
If no, what can I refocus on tomorrow?

Date __/__/__

Rate each on a scale from 1-10 (1=low, 10=high)
 MOOD:___ STRESS:___ ENERGY:___ MOTIVATION:___
Am I satisfied with the work I did today to reach my goals?

☐ YES   ☐ NO

If yes, what helped today?
If no, what can I refocus on tomorrow?

Date __/__/__

Rate each on a scale from 1-10 (1=low, 10=high)
 MOOD:___ STRESS:___ ENERGY:___ MOTIVATION:___
Am I satisfied with the work I did today to reach my goals?

☐ YES   ☐ NO

If yes, what helped today?
If no, what can I refocus on tomorrow?

Date _/_/___

Rate each on a scale from 1-10 (1=low, 10=high)
 MOOD:___ STRESS:___ ENERGY:___ MOTIVATION:___

Am I satisfied with the work I did today to reach my goals?

☐ YES ☐ NO

If yes, what helped today?
If no, what can I refocus on tomorrow?

Date _/_/___

Rate each on a scale from 1-10 (1=low, 10=high)
 MOOD:___ STRESS:___ ENERGY:___ MOTIVATION:___

Am I satisfied with the work I did today to reach my goals?

☐ YES ☐ NO

If yes, what helped today?
If no, what can I refocus on tomorrow?

Date _/_/___

Rate each on a scale from 1-10 (1=low, 10=high)
 MOOD:___ STRESS:___ ENERGY:___ MOTIVATION:___

Am I satisfied with the work I did today to reach my goals?

☐ YES ☐ NO

If yes, what helped today?
If no, what can I refocus on tomorrow?

Date ___/___/___

Weekly Reflection

What emotion have I felt most often this week?

[ ]

Did I take time to notice how I was feeling before or after a big moment?

☐ YES ☐ NO

What was the moment? What did you notice. Whether or not you forgot to pay attention to how you were feeling at the time, how do you feel about it now?

[ ]

Write about a moment that challenged you mentally this week. How did you respond?

[ ]

How intense were your practices or workouts this week? Did anything shift mentally?

[ ]

Read Aloud:

I FOCUS ON WHAT I CAN CONTROL.
I AM PREPARED AND READY.

Week 15
CONFIDENCE THROUGH CONTROL

"You have power over your mind—not outside events. Realize this, and you will find strength."
  - Marcus Aurelius

Athlete Insights: From Blair Stapleton

"There is so much in sports that we cannot control... So, rather than being upset that you can't control those matters, focus on the things you can control—like your attitude and your work ethic. It will save you time, energy, and peace of mind."

Blair learned that confidence isn't about controlling outcomes—it's about controlling effort, attitude, and how you show up. The best athletes don't waste energy on refs, injuries, or other people's opinions. Instead, they pour their focus into what they can improve.

This week is about reclaiming your power. Focus on the parts of the game—and of yourself—that are truly yours.

Confidence grows when you focus on what you can control and let go of what you can't.

Date ___/___/___

Rate each on a scale from 1-10 (1=low, 10=high)
 MOOD:___ STRESS:___ ENERGY:___ MOTIVATION:___
Am I satisfied with the work I did today to reach my goals?

☐ YES ☐ NO

If yes, what helped today?
If no, what can I refocus on tomorrow?

Date ___/___/___

Rate each on a scale from 1-10 (1=low, 10=high)
 MOOD:___ STRESS:___ ENERGY:___ MOTIVATION:___
Am I satisfied with the work I did today to reach my goals?

☐ YES ☐ NO

If yes, what helped today?
If no, what can I refocus on tomorrow?

Date ___/___/___

Rate each on a scale from 1-10 (1=low, 10=high)
 MOOD:___ STRESS:___ ENERGY:___ MOTIVATION:___
Am I satisfied with the work I did today to reach my goals?

☐ YES ☐ NO

If yes, what helped today?
If no, what can I refocus on tomorrow?

Date ___/___/___

Rate each on a scale from 1-10 (1=low, 10=high)
 MOOD:___ STRESS:___ ENERGY:___ MOTIVATION:___

Am I satisfied with the work I did today to reach my goals?

☐ YES   ☐ NO

If yes, what helped today?
If no, what can I refocus on tomorrow?

Date ___/___/___

Rate each on a scale from 1-10 (1=low, 10=high)
 MOOD:___ STRESS:___ ENERGY:___ MOTIVATION:___

Am I satisfied with the work I did today to reach my goals?

☐ YES   ☐ NO

If yes, what helped today?
If no, what can I refocus on tomorrow?

Date ___/___/___

Rate each on a scale from 1-10 (1=low, 10=high)
 MOOD:___ STRESS:___ ENERGY:___ MOTIVATION:___

Am I satisfied with the work I did today to reach my goals?

☐ YES   ☐ NO

If yes, what helped today?
If no, what can I refocus on tomorrow?

Date ___/___/___

Weekly Reflection

What emotion have I felt most often this week?

[ ]

Did I take time to notice how I was feeling before or after a big moment?

☐ YES   ☐ NO

What was the moment? What did you notice. Whether or not you forgot to pay attention to how you were feeling at the time, how do you feel about it now?

[ ]

Write about a moment that challenged you mentally this week. How did you respond?

[ ]

How intense were your practices or workouts this week? Did anything shift mentally?

[ ]

Read Aloud:

I FOCUS ON WHAT I CAN CONTROL.
I AM PREPARED AND READY.

Week 16
STRONG ENOUGH TO SPEAK UP

"What mental health needs is more sunlight, more candor, and more unashamed conversation."

— *Glenn Close*

Athlete Insights: From Blair Stapleton

"After 10+ years of struggling with pretty severe anxiety, I finally got on medication, and it completely changed my life... Life is too short. Say something early. Don't be afraid of the solutions."

Confidence isn't always loud or fearless. Sometimes, it looks like asking for help. Blair's story reminds us that speaking up, getting support, and taking care of your mental health takes more strength than pretending everything is fine.

This week is about embracing your full self. Confidence is not about having it all together—it's about being brave enough to be real.

Confidence means having the courage to speak up when you're struggling.

Date ___/___/___

Rate each on a scale from 1-10 (1=low, 10=high)
  MOOD: ___ STRESS: ___ ENERGY: ___ MOTIVATION: ___

Am I satisfied with the work I did today to reach my goals?

    ☐ YES   ☐ NO

If yes, what helped today?
If no, what can I refocus on tomorrow?

Date ___/___/___

Rate each on a scale from 1-10 (1=low, 10=high)
  MOOD: ___ STRESS: ___ ENERGY: ___ MOTIVATION: ___

Am I satisfied with the work I did today to reach my goals?

    ☐ YES   ☐ NO

If yes, what helped today?
If no, what can I refocus on tomorrow?

Date ___/___/___

Rate each on a scale from 1-10 (1=low, 10=high)
  MOOD: ___ STRESS: ___ ENERGY: ___ MOTIVATION: ___

Am I satisfied with the work I did today to reach my goals?

    ☐ YES   ☐ NO

If yes, what helped today?
If no, what can I refocus on tomorrow?

Date ___/___/___

Rate each on a scale from 1-10 (1=low, 10=high)
 MOOD: ___ STRESS: ___ ENERGY: ___ MOTIVATION: ___

Am I satisfied with the work I did today to reach my goals?

  ☐ YES   ☐ NO

If yes, what helped today?
If no, what can I refocus on tomorrow?

Date ___/___/___

Rate each on a scale from 1-10 (1=low, 10=high)
 MOOD: ___ STRESS: ___ ENERGY: ___ MOTIVATION: ___

Am I satisfied with the work I did today to reach my goals?

  ☐ YES   ☐ NO

If yes, what helped today?
If no, what can I refocus on tomorrow?

Date ___/___/___

Rate each on a scale from 1-10 (1=low, 10=high)
 MOOD: ___ STRESS: ___ ENERGY: ___ MOTIVATION: ___

Am I satisfied with the work I did today to reach my goals?

  ☐ YES   ☐ NO

If yes, what helped today?
If no, what can I refocus on tomorrow?

Date ___/___/___

Weekly Reflection

What emotion have I felt most often this week?

[ ]

Did I take time to notice how I was feeling before or after a big moment?

☐ YES   ☐ NO

What was the moment? What did you notice. Whether or not you forgot to pay attention to how you were feeling at the time, how do you feel about it now?

[ ]

Write about a moment that challenged you mentally this week. How did you respond?

[ ]

How intense were your practices or workouts this week? Did anything shift mentally?

[ ]

Read Aloud:

I FOCUS ON WHAT I CAN CONTROL.
I AM PREPARED AND READY.

MONTH 5
Adaptability

What is Adaptability?

Adaptability is the ability to stay composed and adjust when life doesn't go as planned. For athletes, change is inevitable — an injury, a new coach, a different position, or unexpected adversity. Adaptable athletes respond with clarity, not panic. They find a way to show up with purpose even when the plan shifts.

Adaptability doesn't mean ignoring setbacks or pretending things are easy. It means taking a breath, gathering yourself, and leaning into the challenge with a flexible mindset. Great athletes adapt in real time — they stay grounded in what matters, trust their preparation, and keep learning.

This month, you'll hear from Bo Demarais, a college quarterback from Montana Tech whose approach to leadership, consistency, and mental resets shows how powerful adaptability can be. Whether managing the speed of the game or the weight of expectations, Bo models what it means to stay poised when things don't go your way.

Meet the Athlete:
Bo Demarais

Bo Demarais is a quarterback at Montana Tech University in Butte, Montana. Raised in a sports-minded family, Bo grew up playing baseball, basketball, and football, and developed into one of the most poised and reliable athletes in the state.

At Montana Tech, Bo is known for his leadership, work ethic, and calm presence under pressure. Whether preparing for a game or bouncing back from a tough play, he consistently emphasizes the importance of composure, awareness, and emotional control.

Outside of football, Bo is equally focused on relationships and growth. He brings humility and balance to every aspect of life, drawing strength from faith, family, and his commitment to helping others. His adaptability isn't just about sports — it's how he approaches everything.

Week 17
LEAN INTO THE UNEXPECTED

"The measure of intelligence is the ability to change."
- *Albert Einstein*

Athlete Insights: From Bo Demarais

"Adaptability is everything. When your situation changes, your mindset has to be the first thing that adjusts."

Bo Demarais didn't expect college athletics to come with so many curveballs—injuries, academic changes, shifting positions, and unpredictable team dynamics. At first, the instability felt overwhelming. But over time, Bo realized that adaptability wasn't a backup plan. It was the plan.

He learned to meet change head-on by adjusting his mindset, staying calm in uncertain moments, and building routines that helped him stay steady even when the game—and life—shifted unexpectedly. This week is about embracing that mindset for yourself.

Change is hard, but resisting it is harder. Adaptability is a skill you build through choice, flexibility, and growth.

Date ___/___/___

Rate each on a scale from 1-10 (1=low, 10=high)
  Mood:___ Stress:___ Energy:___ Motivation:___

Am I satisfied with the work I did today to reach my goals?

    ☐ Yes   ☐ No

If yes, what helped today?
If no, what can I refocus on tomorrow?

Date ___/___/___

Rate each on a scale from 1-10 (1=low, 10=high)
  Mood:___ Stress:___ Energy:___ Motivation:___

Am I satisfied with the work I did today to reach my goals?

    ☐ Yes   ☐ No

If yes, what helped today?
If no, what can I refocus on tomorrow?

Date ___/___/___

Rate each on a scale from 1-10 (1=low, 10=high)
  Mood:___ Stress:___ Energy:___ Motivation:___

Am I satisfied with the work I did today to reach my goals?

    ☐ Yes   ☐ No

If yes, what helped today?
If no, what can I refocus on tomorrow?

Date ___/___/___

Rate each on a scale from 1-10 (1=low, 10=high)

MOOD:___ STRESS:___ ENERGY:___ MOTIVATION:___

Am I satisfied with the work I did today to reach my goals?

☐ YES ☐ NO

If yes, what helped today?
If no, what can I refocus on tomorrow?

Date ___/___/___

Rate each on a scale from 1-10 (1=low, 10=high)

MOOD:___ STRESS:___ ENERGY:___ MOTIVATION:___

Am I satisfied with the work I did today to reach my goals?

☐ YES ☐ NO

If yes, what helped today?
If no, what can I refocus on tomorrow?

Date ___/___/___

Rate each on a scale from 1-10 (1=low, 10=high)

MOOD:___ STRESS:___ ENERGY:___ MOTIVATION:___

Am I satisfied with the work I did today to reach my goals?

☐ YES ☐ NO

If yes, what helped today?
If no, what can I refocus on tomorrow?

Date ___/___/___

Weekly Reflection

What emotion have I felt most often this week?

```
[                                                    ]
```

Did I take time to notice how I was feeling before or after a big moment?

☐ YES   ☐ NO

What was the moment? What did you notice. Whether or not you forgot to pay attention to how you were feeling at the time, how do you feel about it now?

```
[                                                    ]
```

Write about a moment that challenged you mentally this week. How did you respond?

```
[                                                    ]
```

How intense were your practices or workouts this week? Did anything shift mentally?

```
[                                                    ]
```

Read Aloud:

I FOCUS ON WHAT I CAN CONTROL.
I AM PREPARED AND READY.

Week 18
MENTAL FLEXIBILTY

> *"Blessed are the flexible, for they shall not be bent out of shape."*
>
> *- Michael McGriffy*

Athlete Insights: From Bo Demarais

"Things don't always go the way you expect. If you let your emotions take over, it becomes hard to think clearly and adjust."

Bo admits he used to let frustration cloud his decisions—whether it was a bad call, a missed play, or something unexpected happening off the field. Over time, he realized that adaptability required not just changing actions, but changing thoughts.

This week is about mental flexibility—the ability to pause, pivot, and rethink when things don't go your way. Athletes with flexible minds make better decisions under pressure and recover faster from setbacks.

Mental flexibility means choosing curiosity over frustration and openness over control.

Date ___/___/___

Rate each on a scale from 1-10 (1=low, 10=high)
 MOOD: ___ STRESS: ___ ENERGY: ___ MOTIVATION: ___

Am I satisfied with the work I did today to reach my goals?

☐ YES   ☐ NO

If yes, what helped today?
If no, what can I refocus on tomorrow?

Date ___/___/___

Rate each on a scale from 1-10 (1=low, 10=high)
 MOOD: ___ STRESS: ___ ENERGY: ___ MOTIVATION: ___

Am I satisfied with the work I did today to reach my goals?

☐ YES   ☐ NO

If yes, what helped today?
If no, what can I refocus on tomorrow?

Date ___/___/___

Rate each on a scale from 1-10 (1=low, 10=high)
 MOOD: ___ STRESS: ___ ENERGY: ___ MOTIVATION: ___

Am I satisfied with the work I did today to reach my goals?

☐ YES   ☐ NO

If yes, what helped today?
If no, what can I refocus on tomorrow?

Date ___/___/___
Rate each on a scale from 1-10 (1=low, 10=high)
  MOOD:___ STRESS:___ ENERGY:___ MOTIVATION:___

Am I satisfied with the work I did today to reach my goals?

☐ YES   ☐ NO

If yes, what helped today?
If no, what can I refocus on tomorrow?

Date ___/___/___
Rate each on a scale from 1-10 (1=low, 10=high)
  MOOD:___ STRESS:___ ENERGY:___ MOTIVATION:___

Am I satisfied with the work I did today to reach my goals?

☐ YES   ☐ NO

If yes, what helped today?
If no, what can I refocus on tomorrow?

Date ___/___/___
Rate each on a scale from 1-10 (1=low, 10=high)
  MOOD:___ STRESS:___ ENERGY:___ MOTIVATION:___

Am I satisfied with the work I did today to reach my goals?

☐ YES   ☐ NO

If yes, what helped today?
If no, what can I refocus on tomorrow?

Date ___/___/___

Weekly Reflection

What emotion have I felt most often this week?

[ ]

Did I take time to notice how I was feeling before or after a big moment?

☐ YES   ☐ NO

What was the moment? What did you notice. Whether or not you forgot to pay attention to how you were feeling at the time, how do you feel about it now?

[ ]

Write about a moment that challenged you mentally this week. How did you respond?

[ ]

How intense were your practices or workouts this week? Did anything shift mentally?

[ ]

Read Aloud:

I FOCUS ON WHAT I CAN CONTROL.
I AM PREPARED AND READY.

Week 19
LEARNING FROM SETBACKS

"Success is not final, failure is not fatal: it is the courage to continue that counts."
- *Winston Churchill*

Athlete Insights: From Bo Demarais

"Every mistake gives you an opportunity to get better. Don't waste it being mad."

Bo realized that beating yourself up over mistakes only delays growth. Instead of spiraling, he started asking better questions: What can I learn? How can I respond? That shift helped him recover faster and take ownership of his development.

This week is about turning setbacks into setups. Mistakes are part of the process—what matters most is how you respond to them.

Mistakes are lessons in disguise. lLean into them, don't run from them.

Date __/__/__

Rate each on a scale from 1-10 (1=low, 10=high)
 MOOD:___ STRESS:___ ENERGY:___ MOTIVATION:___
Am I satisfied with the work I did today to reach my goals?

☐ YES ☐ NO

If yes, what helped today?
If no, what can I refocus on tomorrow?

Date __/__/__

Rate each on a scale from 1-10 (1=low, 10=high)
 MOOD:___ STRESS:___ ENERGY:___ MOTIVATION:___
Am I satisfied with the work I did today to reach my goals?

☐ YES ☐ NO

If yes, what helped today?
If no, what can I refocus on tomorrow?

Date __/__/__

Rate each on a scale from 1-10 (1=low, 10=high)
 MOOD:___ STRESS:___ ENERGY:___ MOTIVATION:___
Am I satisfied with the work I did today to reach my goals?

☐ YES ☐ NO

If yes, what helped today?
If no, what can I refocus on tomorrow?

Date ___/___/___

Rate each on a scale from 1-10 (1=low, 10=high)
 MOOD:___ STRESS:___ ENERGY:___ MOTIVATION:___

Am I satisfied with the work I did today to reach my goals?

☐ YES ☐ NO

If yes, what helped today?
If no, what can I refocus on tomorrow?

Date ___/___/___

Rate each on a scale from 1-10 (1=low, 10=high)
 MOOD:___ STRESS:___ ENERGY:___ MOTIVATION:___

Am I satisfied with the work I did today to reach my goals?

☐ YES ☐ NO

If yes, what helped today?
If no, what can I refocus on tomorrow?

Date ___/___/___

Rate each on a scale from 1-10 (1=low, 10=high)
 MOOD:___ STRESS:___ ENERGY:___ MOTIVATION:___

Am I satisfied with the work I did today to reach my goals?

☐ YES ☐ NO

If yes, what helped today?
If no, what can I refocus on tomorrow?

Date ___/___/___

Weekly Reflection

What emotion have I felt most often this week?

[ ]

Did I take time to notice how I was feeling before or after a big moment?

☐ YES   ☐ NO

What was the moment? What did you notice. Whether or not you forgot to pay attention to how you were feeling at the time, how do you feel about it now?

[ ]

Write about a moment that challenged you mentally this week. How did you respond?

[ ]

How intense were your practices or workouts this week? Did anything shift mentally?

[ ]

Read Aloud:

I FOCUS ON WHAT I CAN CONTROL.
I AM PREPARED AND READY.

Week 20
PERFORMING UNDER PRESSURE

> *"It's not the strongest or the most intelligent who will survive, but those who can best manage change."*
>
> *- Charles Darwin*

Athlete Insights: From Bo Demarais

"The best players adapt—not just to the opponent, but to the moment."

Bo believes that adaptability isn't just physical—it's mental. When the pressure builds, distractions rise, or things don't go as planned, elite athletes don't panic. They adjust. They breathe. They find a new way to contribute.

This week is about sharpening your ability to think, react, and stay present during stressful moments. The more flexible your mindset, the more effective you'll be under pressure.

Pressure reveals what's already inside—train yourself to adapt in any moment.

Date ___/___/___

Rate each on a scale from 1-10 (1=low, 10=high)
   MOOD: ___ STRESS: ___ ENERGY: ___ MOTIVATION: ___

Am I satisfied with the work I did today to reach my goals?

☐ YES ☐ NO

If yes, what helped today?
If no, what can I refocus on tomorrow?

Date ___/___/___

Rate each on a scale from 1-10 (1=low, 10=high)
   MOOD: ___ STRESS: ___ ENERGY: ___ MOTIVATION: ___

Am I satisfied with the work I did today to reach my goals?

☐ YES ☐ NO

If yes, what helped today?
If no, what can I refocus on tomorrow?

Date ___/___/___

Rate each on a scale from 1-10 (1=low, 10=high)
   MOOD: ___ STRESS: ___ ENERGY: ___ MOTIVATION: ___

Am I satisfied with the work I did today to reach my goals?

☐ YES ☐ NO

If yes, what helped today?
If no, what can I refocus on tomorrow?

Date ___/___/___

Rate each on a scale from 1-10 (1=low, 10=high)

MOOD: ___ STRESS: ___ ENERGY: ___ MOTIVATION: ___

Am I satisfied with the work I did today to reach my goals?

☐ YES ☐ NO

If yes, what helped today?
If no, what can I refocus on tomorrow?

Date ___/___/___

Rate each on a scale from 1-10 (1=low, 10=high)

MOOD: ___ STRESS: ___ ENERGY: ___ MOTIVATION: ___

Am I satisfied with the work I did today to reach my goals?

☐ YES ☐ NO

If yes, what helped today?
If no, what can I refocus on tomorrow?

Date ___/___/___

Rate each on a scale from 1-10 (1=low, 10=high)

MOOD: ___ STRESS: ___ ENERGY: ___ MOTIVATION: ___

Am I satisfied with the work I did today to reach my goals?

☐ YES ☐ NO

If yes, what helped today?
If no, what can I refocus on tomorrow?

Date ___/___/___

Weekly Reflection

What emotion have I felt most often this week?

[ ]

Did I take time to notice how I was feeling before or after a big moment?

☐ YES ☐ NO

What was the moment? What did you notice. Whether or not you forgot to pay attention to how you were feeling at the time, how do you feel about it now?

[ ]

Write about a moment that challenged you mentally this week. How did you respond?

[ ]

How intense were your practices or workouts this week? Did anything shift mentally?

[ ]

Read Aloud:

I FOCUS ON WHAT I CAN CONTROL.
I AM PREPARED AND READY.

MONTH 6
Positivity

What is Positivity?

Positivity isn't about pretending everything is perfect. It's about choosing to focus on what's possible, even in hard moments. It's the mindset that sees setbacks as temporary and understands that struggle doesn't mean you're failing. It means you're growing.

In sports, positivity fuels resilience, connection, and joy. It's what allows athletes to smile through nerves, to find gratitude during burnout, and to uplift a teammate even when things aren't going their way.

This month, you'll learn from Brooklyn Griffin, an athlete whose enthusiasm, humor, and honesty make her a powerful example of positive energy. Whether she's leading a chant, supporting a teammate through mental health struggles, or finding joy in "three good things" after a hard day, Brooklyn shows us that positivity is a skill—and one worth practicing.

Meet the Athlete:
> *Brooklyn Griffin*

Brooklyn Griffin has been a standout cheerleader and team leader throughout her athletic career in Great Falls, MT. Known for her vibrant personality, Brooklyn combines passion, mental toughness, and support for her teammates both on and off the mat.

Brooklyn believes that athletes are at their best when they take care of their mental health, talk openly about challenges, and keep perspective in the face of pressure. She has faced injuries, setbacks, and self-doubt, but continues to rise with intention, purpose, and a contagious spirit of gratitude.

Week 21
THE POWER OF DAILY DISCIPLINE

"Positive thinking is not about expecting the best to happen every time, but accepting that whatever happens is the best for this moment."
— *Unknown*

Athlete Insights: From Brooklyn Griffin.

"Just because something feels hard doesn't mean you're failing. Sometimes the hardest days are the ones that shape you the most."

Brooklyn Griffin knows the power of reframing a tough moment. When injuries, burnout, or frustration set in, her instinct is not to shut down—but to reflect, adjust, and keep going. She believes that mental health is directly tied to how you speak to yourself and how you respond when things don't go your way.

This week is about noticing your default mindset. Do you talk to yourself like a critic or a coach? When things go wrong, do you spiral or reset? Positivity isn't pretending everything is okay—it's being honest with yourself while choosing a hopeful response.

This week, notice your thoughts and choose to respond with perspective, not panic.

Date __/__/__

Rate each on a scale from 1-10 (1=low, 10=high)
 MOOD:___ STRESS:___ ENERGY:___ MOTIVATION:___
Am I satisfied with the work I did today to reach my goals?

☐ YES ☐ NO

If yes, what helped today?
If no, what can I refocus on tomorrow?

Date __/__/__

Rate each on a scale from 1-10 (1=low, 10=high)
 MOOD:___ STRESS:___ ENERGY:___ MOTIVATION:___
Am I satisfied with the work I did today to reach my goals?

☐ YES ☐ NO

If yes, what helped today?
If no, what can I refocus on tomorrow?

Date __/__/__

Rate each on a scale from 1-10 (1=low, 10=high)
 MOOD:___ STRESS:___ ENERGY:___ MOTIVATION:___
Am I satisfied with the work I did today to reach my goals?

☐ YES ☐ NO

If yes, what helped today?
If no, what can I refocus on tomorrow?

Date ___/___/___

Rate each on a scale from 1-10 (1=low, 10=high)

MOOD: ___ STRESS: ___ ENERGY: ___ MOTIVATION: ___

Am I satisfied with the work I did today to reach my goals?

☐ YES   ☐ NO

If yes, what helped today?
If no, what can I refocus on tomorrow?

```
┌─────────────────────────────────────────────┐
│                                             │
│                                             │
│                                             │
└─────────────────────────────────────────────┘
```

Date ___/___/___

Rate each on a scale from 1-10 (1=low, 10=high)

MOOD: ___ STRESS: ___ ENERGY: ___ MOTIVATION: ___

Am I satisfied with the work I did today to reach my goals?

☐ YES   ☐ NO

If yes, what helped today?
If no, what can I refocus on tomorrow?

```
┌─────────────────────────────────────────────┐
│                                             │
│                                             │
│                                             │
└─────────────────────────────────────────────┘
```

Date ___/___/___

Rate each on a scale from 1-10 (1=low, 10=high)

MOOD: ___ STRESS: ___ ENERGY: ___ MOTIVATION: ___

Am I satisfied with the work I did today to reach my goals?

☐ YES   ☐ NO

If yes, what helped today?
If no, what can I refocus on tomorrow?

```
┌─────────────────────────────────────────────┐
│                                             │
│                                             │
│                                             │
└─────────────────────────────────────────────┘
```

Date ___/___/___

Weekly Reflection

What emotion have I felt most often this week?

[ ]

Did I take time to notice how I was feeling before or after a big moment?

☐ YES   ☐ NO

What was the moment? What did you notice. Whether or not you forgot to pay attention to how you were feeling at the time, how do you feel about it now?

[ ]

Write about a moment that challenged you mentally this week. How did you respond?

[ ]

How intense were your practices or workouts this week? Did anything shift mentally?

[ ]

Read Aloud:

I FOCUS ON WHAT I CAN CONTROL.
I AM PREPARED AND READY.

Week 22
CHOOSING GRATITUDE

"Gratitude turns what we have into enough."
- Aesop

Athlete Insights: From Brooklyn Griffin.

"When I feel myself getting overwhelmed or stressed, I write down three good things from the day. Even if they are small, like having a good snack or finishing a hard practice, it helps me shift my mindset."

Brooklyn has developed a simple but powerful habit: using gratitude as a reset. Whether it's recovering from a mistake or dealing with pressure, she focuses on finding small wins. This helps her remember that not every day needs to be perfect to be meaningful.

This week, you are invited to practice that same mindset. When things feel tough, train yourself to look for the good. Gratitude doesn't erase challenges, but it gives you a way to carry them with more peace, perspective, and strength.

With gratitude there is room for calm, joy, and perspective, even in hard moments.

Date __/__/__

Rate each on a scale from 1-10 (1=low, 10=high)
 MOOD:___ STRESS:___ ENERGY:___ MOTIVATION:___

Am I satisfied with the work I did today to reach my goals?

☐ YES   ☐ NO

If yes, what helped today?
If no, what can I refocus on tomorrow?

Date __/__/__

Rate each on a scale from 1-10 (1=low, 10=high)
 MOOD:___ STRESS:___ ENERGY:___ MOTIVATION:___

Am I satisfied with the work I did today to reach my goals?

☐ YES   ☐ NO

If yes, what helped today?
If no, what can I refocus on tomorrow?

Date __/__/__

Rate each on a scale from 1-10 (1=low, 10=high)
 MOOD:___ STRESS:___ ENERGY:___ MOTIVATION:___

Am I satisfied with the work I did today to reach my goals?

☐ YES   ☐ NO

If yes, what helped today?
If no, what can I refocus on tomorrow?

Date __/__/__

Rate each on a scale from 1-10 (1=low, 10=high)

MOOD: ___ STRESS: ___ ENERGY: ___ MOTIVATION: ___

Am I satisfied with the work I did today to reach my goals?

☐ YES ☐ NO

If yes, what helped today?
If no, what can I refocus on tomorrow?

Date __/__/__

Rate each on a scale from 1-10 (1=low, 10=high)

MOOD: ___ STRESS: ___ ENERGY: ___ MOTIVATION: ___

Am I satisfied with the work I did today to reach my goals?

☐ YES ☐ NO

If yes, what helped today?
If no, what can I refocus on tomorrow?

Date __/__/__

Rate each on a scale from 1-10 (1=low, 10=high)

MOOD: ___ STRESS: ___ ENERGY: ___ MOTIVATION: ___

Am I satisfied with the work I did today to reach my goals?

☐ YES ☐ NO

If yes, what helped today?
If no, what can I refocus on tomorrow?

Date ___/___/___

Weekly Reflection

What emotion have I felt most often this week?

[ ]

Did I take time to notice how I was feeling before or after a big moment?

☐ YES   ☐ NO

What was the moment? What did you notice. Whether or not you forgot to pay attention to how you were feeling at the time, how do you feel about it now?

[ ]

Write about a moment that challenged you mentally this week. How did you respond?

[ ]

How intense were your practices or workouts this week? Did anything shift mentally?

[ ]

Read Aloud:

I FOCUS ON WHAT I CAN CONTROL.
I AM PREPARED AND READY.

Week 23
POSITIVITY IN LEADERSHIP

"A leader is one who knows the way, goes the way, and shows the way."
— *John C. Maxwell*

Athlete Insights: From Brooklyn Griffin.

"When your energy is good, it's contagious. You never know who needs your positive attitude that day—so lead with it."

Brooklyn believes that positivity isn't just something you use for yourself...it's something you pass on. As a leader, she learned that how she carried herself impacted the entire team. A positive comment, a light-hearted joke, or a simple check-in could change someone's day.

This week is about how you show up for others. Leadership is not about being perfect or always upbeat. It's about choosing to set the tone, especially when things are tough. A positive presence can be the difference between a disconnected team and one that lifts each other up.

Positivity in leadership means using your energy to create space for others to feel seen, supported, and encouraged.

Date ___/___/___

Rate each on a scale from 1-10 (1=low, 10=high)
 MOOD:___ STRESS:___ ENERGY:___ MOTIVATION:___
Am I satisfied with the work I did today to reach my goals?

☐ YES ☐ NO

If yes, what helped today?
If no, what can I refocus on tomorrow?

Date ___/___/___

Rate each on a scale from 1-10 (1=low, 10=high)
 MOOD:___ STRESS:___ ENERGY:___ MOTIVATION:___
Am I satisfied with the work I did today to reach my goals?

☐ YES ☐ NO

If yes, what helped today?
If no, what can I refocus on tomorrow?

Date ___/___/___

Rate each on a scale from 1-10 (1=low, 10=high)
 MOOD:___ STRESS:___ ENERGY:___ MOTIVATION:___
Am I satisfied with the work I did today to reach my goals?

☐ YES ☐ NO

If yes, what helped today?
If no, what can I refocus on tomorrow?

Date ___/___/___

Rate each on a scale from 1-10 (1=low, 10=high)
 MOOD:___ STRESS:___ ENERGY:___ MOTIVATION:___

Am I satisfied with the work I did today to reach my goals?

☐ YES   ☐ NO

If yes, what helped today?
If no, what can I refocus on tomorrow?

Date ___/___/___

Rate each on a scale from 1-10 (1=low, 10=high)
 MOOD:___ STRESS:___ ENERGY:___ MOTIVATION:___

Am I satisfied with the work I did today to reach my goals?

☐ YES   ☐ NO

If yes, what helped today?
If no, what can I refocus on tomorrow?

Date ___/___/___

Rate each on a scale from 1-10 (1=low, 10=high)
 MOOD:___ STRESS:___ ENERGY:___ MOTIVATION:___

Am I satisfied with the work I did today to reach my goals?

☐ YES   ☐ NO

If yes, what helped today?
If no, what can I refocus on tomorrow?

Date __/__/____

Weekly Reflection

What emotion have I felt most often this week?

[   ]

Did I take time to notice how I was feeling before or after a big moment?

☐ YES   ☐ NO

What was the moment? What did you notice. Whether or not you forgot to pay attention to how you were feeling at the time, how do you feel about it now?

[   ]

Write about a moment that challenged you mentally this week. How did you respond?

[   ]

How intense were your practices or workouts this week? Did anything shift mentally?

[   ]

Read Aloud:

I FOCUS ON WHAT I CAN CONTROL.
I AM PREPARED AND READY.

Week 24
POSITIVITY AS PERSPECTIVE

"Positive anything is better than negative nothing."

- Elbert Hubbard

Athlete Insights: From Brooklyn Griffin.

"Even when I was injured, I had to find a way to stay positive. I reminded myself to be grateful for what I still had—my team, my knowledge of the game, and my opportunity to grow."

Brooklyn's experience with injury tested her ability to stay positive. It forced her to reframe what it meant to contribute. Instead of focusing on what she could no longer do, she focused on what she could still offer.

This week is about redefining what success and progress look like. Sometimes the most important step is perspective. Like choosing to look at the situation in a new way. Even when setbacks happen, you still have value, and you still have options.

Positivity is not about pretending everything is okay. It is about choosing to look for what still matters and what you can still give.

Date ___/___/___

Rate each on a scale from 1-10 (1=low, 10=high)
  MOOD:___ STRESS:___ ENERGY:___ MOTIVATION:___

Am I satisfied with the work I did today to reach my goals?

☐ YES   ☐ NO

If yes, what helped today?
If no, what can I refocus on tomorrow?

```
┌─────────────────────────────────────────┐
│                                         │
│                                         │
│                                         │
└─────────────────────────────────────────┘
```

Date ___/___/___

Rate each on a scale from 1-10 (1=low, 10=high)
  MOOD:___ STRESS:___ ENERGY:___ MOTIVATION:___

Am I satisfied with the work I did today to reach my goals?

☐ YES   ☐ NO

If yes, what helped today?
If no, what can I refocus on tomorrow?

```
┌─────────────────────────────────────────┐
│                                         │
│                                         │
│                                         │
└─────────────────────────────────────────┘
```

Date ___/___/___

Rate each on a scale from 1-10 (1=low, 10=high)
  MOOD:___ STRESS:___ ENERGY:___ MOTIVATION:___

Am I satisfied with the work I did today to reach my goals?

☐ YES   ☐ NO

If yes, what helped today?
If no, what can I refocus on tomorrow?

```
┌─────────────────────────────────────────┐
│                                         │
│                                         │
│                                         │
└─────────────────────────────────────────┘
```

Date ___/___/___
Rate each on a scale from 1-10 (1=low, 10=high)
  MOOD:___ STRESS:___ ENERGY:___ MOTIVATION:___
Am I satisfied with the work I did today to reach my goals?

☐ YES   ☐ NO

If yes, what helped today?
If no, what can I refocus on tomorrow?

Date ___/___/___
Rate each on a scale from 1-10 (1=low, 10=high)
  MOOD:___ STRESS:___ ENERGY:___ MOTIVATION:___
Am I satisfied with the work I did today to reach my goals?

☐ YES   ☐ NO

If yes, what helped today?
If no, what can I refocus on tomorrow?

Date ___/___/___
Rate each on a scale from 1-10 (1=low, 10=high)
  MOOD:___ STRESS:___ ENERGY:___ MOTIVATION:___
Am I satisfied with the work I did today to reach my goals?

☐ YES   ☐ NO

If yes, what helped today?
If no, what can I refocus on tomorrow?

Date ___/___/___

Weekly Reflection

What emotion have I felt most often this week?

[ ]

Did I take time to notice how I was feeling before or after a big moment?

☐ YES ☐ NO

What was the moment? What did you notice. Whether or not you forgot to pay attention to how you were feeling at the time, how do you feel about it now?

[ ]

Write about a moment that challenged you mentally this week. How did you respond?

[ ]

How intense were your practices or workouts this week? Did anything shift mentally?

[ ]

Read Aloud:

I FOCUS ON WHAT I CAN CONTROL.
I AM PREPARED AND READY.

MONTH 7
Leadership

What is Leadership?

Leadership in sports is not about having the loudest voice in the room or being the most talented player on the field. It is about how you influence others—through your actions, your mindset, and your ability to make people around you better.

A great leader leads by example. They stay calm under pressure, they own their mistakes, and they lift up teammates when things go sideways. Leadership also means being willing to have hard conversations, take accountability, and stay aligned with the team's bigger purpose.

This month, you will learn from Jared Zabransky, a quarterback who led Boise State to one of the most iconic wins in college football history and went on to compete professionally in the CFL. Jared's story is one of mental toughness, poise under pressure, and the type of leadership that turns belief into action.

Meet the Athlete:
> *Jared Zobransky*

Jared Zabransky is best known for leading the Boise State Broncos to a dramatic 2007 Fiesta Bowl victory over the Oklahoma Sooners, a game widely regarded as one of the greatest in college football history. Jared threw for over 8,000 yards in his college career and was named the game's Offensive MVP.

After Boise State, Jared signed with the Houston Texans before moving on to the Canadian Football League, where he played quarterback for the Edmonton Eskimos.

Today, Jared is a successful business leader and motivational speaker. He brings the same competitive edge, mental discipline, and leadership skills to his post-athletic career, mentoring others on how to thrive in high-stakes environments.

Week 25
LEADING BY EXAMPLE

"Leadership is practiced not so much in words as in attitude and in actions."
— *Harold Geneen*

Athlete Insights: From Jared Zabransky.

"If I can't get myself locked in first, how can I expect anyone else to trust me in the huddle?"

Jared Zabransky knew the pressure that came with being a quarterback. Before he ever stepped into the huddle, he had to show his team that he was prepared, focused, and ready to lead. That started with his own habits. Film study. Practice. Composure.

Leadership, for Jared, was not about talking the loudest or giving the best speech. It was about consistency. It was about bringing the same energy every day, no matter the scoreboard or the noise. When people see your effort and focus, they begin to believe in you. That is when real leadership begins.

Others take their cues from how you show up. Be the example you want to follow.

Date ___/___/___

Rate each on a scale from 1-10 (1=low, 10=high)
 Mood:___ Stress:___ Energy:___ Motivation:___

Am I satisfied with the work I did today to reach my goals?

☐ Yes ☐ No

If yes, what helped today?
If no, what can I refocus on tomorrow?

Date ___/___/___

Rate each on a scale from 1-10 (1=low, 10=high)
 Mood:___ Stress:___ Energy:___ Motivation:___

Am I satisfied with the work I did today to reach my goals?

☐ Yes ☐ No

If yes, what helped today?
If no, what can I refocus on tomorrow?

Date ___/___/___

Rate each on a scale from 1-10 (1=low, 10=high)
 Mood:___ Stress:___ Energy:___ Motivation:___

Am I satisfied with the work I did today to reach my goals?

☐ Yes ☐ No

If yes, what helped today?
If no, what can I refocus on tomorrow?

Date ___/___/___

Rate each on a scale from 1-10 (1=low, 10=high)
   MOOD:___ STRESS:___ ENERGY:___ MOTIVATION:___

Am I satisfied with the work I did today to reach my goals?

☐ YES   ☐ NO

If yes, what helped today?
If no, what can I refocus on tomorrow?

Date ___/___/___

Rate each on a scale from 1-10 (1=low, 10=high)
   MOOD:___ STRESS:___ ENERGY:___ MOTIVATION:___

Am I satisfied with the work I did today to reach my goals?

☐ YES   ☐ NO

If yes, what helped today?
If no, what can I refocus on tomorrow?

Date ___/___/___

Rate each on a scale from 1-10 (1=low, 10=high)
   MOOD:___ STRESS:___ ENERGY:___ MOTIVATION:___

Am I satisfied with the work I did today to reach my goals?

☐ YES   ☐ NO

If yes, what helped today?
If no, what can I refocus on tomorrow?

Date ___/___/___

Weekly Reflection

What emotion have I felt most often this week?

[ ]

Did I take time to notice how I was feeling before or after a big moment?

☐ YES   ☐ NO

What was the moment? What did you notice. Whether or not you forgot to pay attention to how you were feeling at the time, how do you feel about it now?

[ ]

Write about a moment that challenged you mentally this week. How did you respond?

[ ]

How intense were your practices or workouts this week? Did anything shift mentally?

[ ]

Read Aloud:

**I FOCUS ON WHAT I CAN CONTROL.
I AM PREPARED AND READY.**

Week 26
LEADERSHIP THROUGH ADVERSITY

"Anyone can hold the helm when the sea is calm."
- Publilius Syrus

Athlete Insights: From Jared Zabransky.

"When I made mistakes, I owned them. That is part of being a quarterback. You cannot hide. The team needs to know you are accountable."

Jared's journey was not all touchdowns and trophies. During his senior year at Boise State, he faced national criticism after a tough bowl game loss. But he refused to point fingers. Instead, he took ownership of the mistakes and used them to fuel his growth. That moment helped define his leadership.

Great leaders do not pretend to be perfect. They take responsibility. They learn out loud. And they inspire others by staying steady when things go wrong. This week is about showing up with courage, even when it is uncomfortable.

Leadership is revealed in how you respond when things go wrong.

Date ___/___/___

Rate each on a scale from 1-10 (1=low, 10=high)
  Mood:___ Stress:___ Energy:___ Motivation:___
Am I satisfied with the work I did today to reach my goals?

☐ Yes   ☐ No

If yes, what helped today?
If no, what can I refocus on tomorrow?

```
┌────────────────────────────────────────┐
│                                        │
│                                        │
└────────────────────────────────────────┘
```

Date ___/___/___

Rate each on a scale from 1-10 (1=low, 10=high)
  Mood:___ Stress:___ Energy:___ Motivation:___
Am I satisfied with the work I did today to reach my goals?

☐ Yes   ☐ No

If yes, what helped today?
If no, what can I refocus on tomorrow?

```
┌────────────────────────────────────────┐
│                                        │
│                                        │
└────────────────────────────────────────┘
```

Date ___/___/___

Rate each on a scale from 1-10 (1=low, 10=high)
  Mood:___ Stress:___ Energy:___ Motivation:___
Am I satisfied with the work I did today to reach my goals?

☐ Yes   ☐ No

If yes, what helped today?
If no, what can I refocus on tomorrow?

```
┌────────────────────────────────────────┐
│                                        │
│                                        │
└────────────────────────────────────────┘
```

Date ___/___/___

Rate each on a scale from 1-10 (1=low, 10=high)
MOOD: ___ STRESS: ___ ENERGY: ___ MOTIVATION: ___

Am I satisfied with the work I did today to reach my goals?

☐ YES   ☐ NO

If yes, what helped today?
If no, what can I refocus on tomorrow?

Date ___/___/___

Rate each on a scale from 1-10 (1=low, 10=high)
MOOD: ___ STRESS: ___ ENERGY: ___ MOTIVATION: ___

Am I satisfied with the work I did today to reach my goals?

☐ YES   ☐ NO

If yes, what helped today?
If no, what can I refocus on tomorrow?

Date ___/___/___

Rate each on a scale from 1-10 (1=low, 10=high)
MOOD: ___ STRESS: ___ ENERGY: ___ MOTIVATION: ___

Am I satisfied with the work I did today to reach my goals?

☐ YES   ☐ NO

If yes, what helped today?
If no, what can I refocus on tomorrow?

Date ___/___/___

Weekly Reflection

What emotion have I felt most often this week?

[ ]

Did I take time to notice how I was feeling before or after a big moment?

☐ YES   ☐ NO

What was the moment? What did you notice. Whether or not you forgot to pay attention to how you were feeling at the time, how do you feel about it now?

[ ]

Write about a moment that challenged you mentally this week. How did you respond?

[ ]

How intense were your practices or workouts this week? Did anything shift mentally?

[ ]

Read Aloud:

I FOCUS ON WHAT I CAN CONTROL.
I AM PREPARED AND READY.

PREPARATION

"Success depends upon previous preparation, and without such preparation there is sure to be failure."

— *Confucius*

Athlete Insights: From Jared Zabransky.

"I always tried to out-prepare the other guy. If you are the most prepared, you will be the most confident. And you will lead by example."

Jared believes the best leaders are not always the loudest. They are often the ones who stay late, study the game plan, and do the little things right every day. He understood that leadership starts before the game ever begins.

In football and in life, preparation is a signal of respect. It shows your team you care. It tells your coaches they can trust you. It builds confidence that spreads. This week is about using preparation as a tool to lead others and to lead yourself.

Preparation is one of the clearest ways to lead without saying a word.

Date ___/___/___

Rate each on a scale from 1-10 (1=low, 10=high)
  MOOD: ___ STRESS: ___ ENERGY: ___ MOTIVATION: ___

Am I satisfied with the work I did today to reach my goals?

☐ YES ☐ NO

If yes, what helped today?
If no, what can I refocus on tomorrow?

Date ___/___/___

Rate each on a scale from 1-10 (1=low, 10=high)
  MOOD: ___ STRESS: ___ ENERGY: ___ MOTIVATION: ___

Am I satisfied with the work I did today to reach my goals?

☐ YES ☐ NO

If yes, what helped today?
If no, what can I refocus on tomorrow?

Date ___/___/___

Rate each on a scale from 1-10 (1=low, 10=high)
  MOOD: ___ STRESS: ___ ENERGY: ___ MOTIVATION: ___

Am I satisfied with the work I did today to reach my goals?

☐ YES ☐ NO

If yes, what helped today?
If no, what can I refocus on tomorrow?

Date ___/___/___

Rate each on a scale from 1-10 (1=low, 10=high)

MOOD:___ STRESS:___ ENERGY:___ MOTIVATION:___

Am I satisfied with the work I did today to reach my goals?

☐ YES ☐ NO

If yes, what helped today?
If no, what can I refocus on tomorrow?

Date ___/___/___

Rate each on a scale from 1-10 (1=low, 10=high)

MOOD:___ STRESS:___ ENERGY:___ MOTIVATION:___

Am I satisfied with the work I did today to reach my goals?

☐ YES ☐ NO

If yes, what helped today?
If no, what can I refocus on tomorrow?

Date ___/___/___

Rate each on a scale from 1-10 (1=low, 10=high)

MOOD:___ STRESS:___ ENERGY:___ MOTIVATION:___

Am I satisfied with the work I did today to reach my goals?

☐ YES ☐ NO

If yes, what helped today?
If no, what can I refocus on tomorrow?

Date ___/___/___

Weekly Reflection

What emotion have I felt most often this week?

[   ]

Did I take time to notice how I was feeling before or after a big moment?

☐ YES   ☐ NO

What was the moment? What did you notice. Whether or not you forgot to pay attention to how you were feeling at the time, how do you feel about it now?

[   ]

Write about a moment that challenged you mentally this week. How did you respond?

[   ]

How intense were your practices or workouts this week? Did anything shift mentally?

[   ]

Read Aloud:

I FOCUS ON WHAT I CAN CONTROL.
I AM PREPARED AND READY.

Week 28
CHARACTER MATTERS

"The true test of a man's character is what he does when no one is watching."
— John Wooden

Athlete Insights: From Jared Zabransky.

"Be someone people can count on. Your words, your actions, your energy. People are always watching, even when you do not know it."

For Jared, leadership was never just about performance. It was about integrity. It was about showing up with respect for the game, for your teammates, and for yourself. Leadership shows up in your character long before it shows up on a scoreboard.

Athletes who lead with character stay consistent, even when no one is watching. They treat others with respect, win or lose. They own their mistakes. That kind of leadership builds trust and changes teams from the inside out.

Your actions shape the culture around you. Make them count.

Date ___/___/___

Rate each on a scale from 1-10 (1=low, 10=high)
  MOOD:___ STRESS:___ ENERGY:___ MOTIVATION:___

Am I satisfied with the work I did today to reach my goals?

☐ YES   ☐ NO

If yes, what helped today?
If no, what can I refocus on tomorrow?

Date ___/___/___

Rate each on a scale from 1-10 (1=low, 10=high)
  MOOD:___ STRESS:___ ENERGY:___ MOTIVATION:___

Am I satisfied with the work I did today to reach my goals?

☐ YES   ☐ NO

If yes, what helped today?
If no, what can I refocus on tomorrow?

Date ___/___/___

Rate each on a scale from 1-10 (1=low, 10=high)
  MOOD:___ STRESS:___ ENERGY:___ MOTIVATION:___

Am I satisfied with the work I did today to reach my goals?

☐ YES   ☐ NO

If yes, what helped today?
If no, what can I refocus on tomorrow?

Date ___/___/___

Rate each on a scale from 1-10 (1=low, 10=high)
 MOOD:___ STRESS:___ ENERGY:___ MOTIVATION:___
Am I satisfied with the work I did today to reach my goals?

☐ YES ☐ NO

If yes, what helped today?
If no, what can I refocus on tomorrow?

Date ___/___/___

Rate each on a scale from 1-10 (1=low, 10=high)
 MOOD:___ STRESS:___ ENERGY:___ MOTIVATION:___
Am I satisfied with the work I did today to reach my goals?

☐ YES ☐ NO

If yes, what helped today?
If no, what can I refocus on tomorrow?

Date ___/___/___

Rate each on a scale from 1-10 (1=low, 10=high)
 MOOD:___ STRESS:___ ENERGY:___ MOTIVATION:___
Am I satisfied with the work I did today to reach my goals?

☐ YES ☐ NO

If yes, what helped today?
If no, what can I refocus on tomorrow?

Date ___/___/___

Weekly Reflection

What emotion have I felt most often this week?

[ ]

Did I take time to notice how I was feeling before or after a big moment?

☐ YES   ☐ NO

What was the moment? What did you notice. Whether or not you forgot to pay attention to how you were feeling at the time, how do you feel about it now?

[ ]

Write about a moment that challenged you mentally this week. How did you respond?

[ ]

How intense were your practices or workouts this week? Did anything shift mentally?

[ ]

Read Aloud:

I FOCUS ON WHAT I CAN CONTROL.
I AM PREPARED AND READY.

MONTH 8
Accountability

What is Accountability?

Accountability is the ability to take ownership of your actions, your choices, and your role on the team. It is not just about showing up, but about being someone others can depend on. It means recognizing your mistakes, learning from them, and committing to growth.

In sports, accountability separates good athletes from great ones. It shows up in your preparation, your communication, and your consistency. It is holding yourself to a high standard, even when no one is watching.

This month, you will learn from David Smith, a former All-Big Sky football standout at Montana State University. David's journey shows how accountability is built through action, leadership, and a refusal to make excuses. His insights reveal how owning your role and your effort can create trust, respect, and long-term success.

Meet the Athlete:
David Smith

David Smith was among the first players to sign with Montana State University after Coach Mike Kramer took over the program in 2000. Smith made an immediate impact, playing in all 11 games during his first season and starting as a sophomore. By 2002, he was a key piece of the Bobcats' defense and helped lead the team to its first championship in 18 years.

Known for his versatility, intelligence, and toughness, David was the perfect complement to MSU's physical secondary. He earned Second Team All-Big Sky honors as a senior and was respected for his leadership both on and off the field

Today, David continues to lead by example in his professional life and personal relationships. He is a husband, a father, and a mentor who lives out the same accountability he brought to the football field.

Week 29
ACCOUNTABILITY IS YOURS

"The price of greatness is responsibility."
- Winston Churchill

Athlete Insights: From David Smith.

"You cannot expect someone to lead you if you are not willing to lead yourself."

David Smith learned early that accountability is a personal decision. Before you can lead a team or earn respect from coaches and peers, you have to take responsibility for your own habits. For David, that meant being honest with himself, working on the small things, and taking pride in preparation.

When you take ownership of your effort and attitude, you create momentum. Accountability is not about being perfect. It is about showing up, staying honest, and learning from the moments when you fall short. This week is about holding yourself to the standard you want others to follow.

Your goals mean nothing without the discipline to follow through.

Date __/__/__

Rate each on a scale from 1-10 (1=low, 10=high)
 MOOD:___ STRESS:___ ENERGY:___ MOTIVATION:___
Am I satisfied with the work I did today to reach my goals?

☐ YES ☐ NO

If yes, what helped today?
If no, what can I refocus on tomorrow?

Date __/__/__

Rate each on a scale from 1-10 (1=low, 10=high)
 MOOD:___ STRESS:___ ENERGY:___ MOTIVATION:___
Am I satisfied with the work I did today to reach my goals?

☐ YES ☐ NO

If yes, what helped today?
If no, what can I refocus on tomorrow?

Date __/__/__

Rate each on a scale from 1-10 (1=low, 10=high)
 MOOD:___ STRESS:___ ENERGY:___ MOTIVATION:___
Am I satisfied with the work I did today to reach my goals?

☐ YES ☐ NO

If yes, what helped today?
If no, what can I refocus on tomorrow?

Date ___/___/___

Rate each on a scale from 1-10 (1=low, 10=high)

  Mood: ___ Stress: ___ Energy: ___ Motivation: ___

Am I satisfied with the work I did today to reach my goals?

    ☐ Yes   ☐ No

If yes, what helped today?
If no, what can I refocus on tomorrow?

Date ___/___/___

Rate each on a scale from 1-10 (1=low, 10=high)

  Mood: ___ Stress: ___ Energy: ___ Motivation: ___

Am I satisfied with the work I did today to reach my goals?

    ☐ Yes   ☐ No

If yes, what helped today?
If no, what can I refocus on tomorrow?

Date ___/___/___

Rate each on a scale from 1-10 (1=low, 10=high)

  Mood: ___ Stress: ___ Energy: ___ Motivation: ___

Am I satisfied with the work I did today to reach my goals?

    ☐ Yes   ☐ No

If yes, what helped today?
If no, what can I refocus on tomorrow?

Date ___/___/___

Weekly Reflection

What emotion have I felt most often this week?

[ ]

Did I take time to notice how I was feeling before or after a big moment?

☐ YES ☐ NO

What was the moment? What did you notice. Whether or not you forgot to pay attention to how you were feeling at the time, how do you feel about it now?

[ ]

Write about a moment that challenged you mentally this week. How did you respond?

[ ]

How intense were your practices or workouts this week? Did anything shift mentally?

[ ]

Read Aloud:

I FOCUS ON WHAT I CAN CONTROL.
I AM PREPARED AND READY.

Week 30
DEAL WITH THE DETAILS

"Success is the sum of small efforts repeated day in and day out."

- Robert Collier

Athlete Insights: From David Smith.

"My advice to a younger version of me would be to focus on the little things. The details add up. You may not see it now, but if you do the right thing over and over, good things will come."

David's story is a reminder that greatness is not built on big moments. It is built on habits. The best athletes do not just show up for game day. They show up for the warmups, the early reps, the recovery sessions, and the quiet choices that no one else sees.

Accountability starts with discipline in the smallest areas. How you tape your ankles, how you talk to yourself when no one is around, how you react when things are not going your way. These moments define your path more than any highlight reel.

The little things are the big things. Every choice matters.

Date ___/___/___

Rate each on a scale from 1-10 (1=low, 10=high)

MOOD: ___ STRESS: ___ ENERGY: ___ MOTIVATION: ___

Am I satisfied with the work I did today to reach my goals?

☐ YES   ☐ NO

If yes, what helped today?
If no, what can I refocus on tomorrow?

Date ___/___/___

Rate each on a scale from 1-10 (1=low, 10=high)

MOOD: ___ STRESS: ___ ENERGY: ___ MOTIVATION: ___

Am I satisfied with the work I did today to reach my goals?

☐ YES   ☐ NO

If yes, what helped today?
If no, what can I refocus on tomorrow?

Date ___/___/___

Rate each on a scale from 1-10 (1=low, 10=high)

MOOD: ___ STRESS: ___ ENERGY: ___ MOTIVATION: ___

Am I satisfied with the work I did today to reach my goals?

☐ YES   ☐ NO

If yes, what helped today?
If no, what can I refocus on tomorrow?

Date ___/___/___

Rate each on a scale from 1-10 (1=low, 10=high)

MOOD:___ STRESS:___ ENERGY:___ MOTIVATION:___

Am I satisfied with the work I did today to reach my goals?

☐ YES   ☐ NO

If yes, what helped today?
If no, what can I refocus on tomorrow?

Date ___/___/___

Rate each on a scale from 1-10 (1=low, 10=high)

MOOD:___ STRESS:___ ENERGY:___ MOTIVATION:___

Am I satisfied with the work I did today to reach my goals?

☐ YES   ☐ NO

If yes, what helped today?
If no, what can I refocus on tomorrow?

Date ___/___/___

Rate each on a scale from 1-10 (1=low, 10=high)

MOOD:___ STRESS:___ ENERGY:___ MOTIVATION:___

Am I satisfied with the work I did today to reach my goals?

☐ YES   ☐ NO

If yes, what helped today?
If no, what can I refocus on tomorrow?

Date __/__/__

Weekly Reflection

What emotion have I felt most often this week?

[ ]

Did I take time to notice how I was feeling before or after a big moment?

☐ YES   ☐ NO

What was the moment? What did you notice. Whether or not you forgot to pay attention to how you were feeling at the time, how do you feel about it now?

[ ]

Write about a moment that challenged you mentally this week. How did you respond?

[ ]

How intense were your practices or workouts this week? Did anything shift mentally?

[ ]

Read Aloud:

I FOCUS ON WHAT I CAN CONTROL.
I AM PREPARED AND READY.

Week 31
YOUR TEAM NEEDS YOU

"The strength of the team is each individual member. The strength of each member is the team."

— *Phil Jackson*

Athlete Insights: From David Smith.

"It is not about individual success. If you want to grow, you have to show up for your teammates. The better they get, the better you get."

David's time in football taught him a deep truth about leadership. You are not accountable only for your own actions. You are also responsible for how you support, challenge, and encourage the people around you. Great teams are built when every player takes ownership of their role and lifts the group.

This kind of accountability is not just about talent. It is about showing up on time, keeping your word, and making the people around you better. It means giving energy, not just taking it. It means leading with action, not just words.

When you commit to others, you play with more purpose.

Date ___/___/___

Rate each on a scale from 1-10 (1=low, 10=high)
  MOOD: ___ STRESS: ___ ENERGY: ___ MOTIVATION: ___
Am I satisfied with the work I did today to reach my goals?

☐ YES ☐ NO

If yes, what helped today?
If no, what can I refocus on tomorrow?

Date ___/___/___

Rate each on a scale from 1-10 (1=low, 10=high)
  MOOD: ___ STRESS: ___ ENERGY: ___ MOTIVATION: ___
Am I satisfied with the work I did today to reach my goals?

☐ YES ☐ NO

If yes, what helped today?
If no, what can I refocus on tomorrow?

Date ___/___/___

Rate each on a scale from 1-10 (1=low, 10=high)
  MOOD: ___ STRESS: ___ ENERGY: ___ MOTIVATION: ___
Am I satisfied with the work I did today to reach my goals?

☐ YES ☐ NO

If yes, what helped today?
If no, what can I refocus on tomorrow?

Date ___/___/___

Rate each on a scale from 1-10 (1=low, 10=high)
  MOOD:___ STRESS:___ ENERGY:___ MOTIVATION:___

Am I satisfied with the work I did today to reach my goals?

☐ YES ☐ NO

If yes, what helped today?
If no, what can I refocus on tomorrow?

Date ___/___/___

Rate each on a scale from 1-10 (1=low, 10=high)
  MOOD:___ STRESS:___ ENERGY:___ MOTIVATION:___

Am I satisfied with the work I did today to reach my goals?

☐ YES ☐ NO

If yes, what helped today?
If no, what can I refocus on tomorrow?

Date ___/___/___

Rate each on a scale from 1-10 (1=low, 10=high)
  MOOD:___ STRESS:___ ENERGY:___ MOTIVATION:___

Am I satisfied with the work I did today to reach my goals?

☐ YES ☐ NO

If yes, what helped today?
If no, what can I refocus on tomorrow?

Date ___/___/___

Weekly Reflection

What emotion have I felt most often this week?

[ ]

Did I take time to notice how I was feeling before or after a big moment?

☐ YES   ☐ NO

What was the moment? What did you notice. Whether or not you forgot to pay attention to how you were feeling at the time, how do you feel about it now?

[ ]

Write about a moment that challenged you mentally this week. How did you respond?

[ ]

How intense were your practices or workouts this week? Did anything shift mentally?

[ ]

Read Aloud:
I FOCUS ON WHAT I CAN CONTROL.
I AM PREPARED AND READY.

Week 32
FINISHING WITH PURPOSE

"If you only work on the days you feel good, you will not get very far."
— Jerry West

Athlete Insights: From David Smith.

"Every day is an opportunity to sharpen your tools. When you look at your day like that, even the boring or hard parts matter."

Discipline is not just about starting strong. It is about finishing well, even when your motivation fades. David credits his long career to his consistency. Whether he was the star or a role player, whether he was training in January or competing in July, he stayed committed to the process.

This week, we focus on what it means to finish with purpose. Discipline is built in the last reps, the late nights, and the moments when it would be easier to coast.

Finishing strong is a habit that separates those who want it from those who live it.

Date __/__/__

Rate each on a scale from 1-10 (1=low, 10=high)
 MOOD:___ STRESS:___ ENERGY:___ MOTIVATION:___

Am I satisfied with the work I did today to reach my goals?

☐ YES   ☐ NO

If yes, what helped today?
If no, what can I refocus on tomorrow?

Date __/__/__

Rate each on a scale from 1-10 (1=low, 10=high)
 MOOD:___ STRESS:___ ENERGY:___ MOTIVATION:___

Am I satisfied with the work I did today to reach my goals?

☐ YES   ☐ NO

If yes, what helped today?
If no, what can I refocus on tomorrow?

Date __/__/__

Rate each on a scale from 1-10 (1=low, 10=high)
 MOOD:___ STRESS:___ ENERGY:___ MOTIVATION:___

Am I satisfied with the work I did today to reach my goals?

☐ YES   ☐ NO

If yes, what helped today?
If no, what can I refocus on tomorrow?

Date ___/___/___

Rate each on a scale from 1-10 (1=low, 10=high)
 MOOD:___ STRESS:___ ENERGY:___ MOTIVATION:___

Am I satisfied with the work I did today to reach my goals?

☐ YES ☐ NO

If yes, what helped today?
If no, what can I refocus on tomorrow?

Date ___/___/___

Rate each on a scale from 1-10 (1=low, 10=high)
 MOOD:___ STRESS:___ ENERGY:___ MOTIVATION:___

Am I satisfied with the work I did today to reach my goals?

☐ YES ☐ NO

If yes, what helped today?
If no, what can I refocus on tomorrow?

Date ___/___/___

Rate each on a scale from 1-10 (1=low, 10=high)
 MOOD:___ STRESS:___ ENERGY:___ MOTIVATION:___

Am I satisfied with the work I did today to reach my goals?

☐ YES ☐ NO

If yes, what helped today?
If no, what can I refocus on tomorrow?

Date ___/___/___

Weekly Reflection

What emotion have I felt most often this week?

[ ]

Did I take time to notice how I was feeling before or after a big moment?

☐ YES ☐ NO

What was the moment? What did you notice. Whether or not you forgot to pay attention to how you were feeling at the time, how do you feel about it now?

[ ]

Write about a moment that challenged you mentally this week. How did you respond?

[ ]

How intense were your practices or workouts this week? Did anything shift mentally?

[ ]

Read Aloud:

I FOCUS ON WHAT I CAN CONTROL.
I AM PREPARED AND READY.

MONTH 9
Conviction

What is Conviction?

Conviction is the deep belief that guides your actions when things get hard. It is knowing why you show up and staying committed to that reason even when motivation fades, pressure builds, or uncertainty creeps in. Conviction is not loud confidence. It is steady purpose.

Athletes with conviction do not rely on emotions to carry them forward. They rely on values, preparation, and clarity. Conviction shows up in the choices you make when no one is watching, in the way you respond to adversity, and in your willingness to keep moving forward even when the path is uncomfortable.

This month, you will learn from Matt Brownlow, a former Montana State football player whose journey highlights the power of belief, preparation, community, and mental discipline.

Meet the Athlete:

Matt Brownlow

Matt Brownlow is a former Montana State University football player and a graduate of Missoula Sentinel High School. Known as one of the hardest-working and most approachable Bobcats in the program, Matt built his career on resilience, discipline, and consistency. His decision to continue pursuing what once felt like an impossible dream became one of the most rewarding choices of his life.

Today, Matt brings the same mindset into his professional career as a business consultant with a background in marketing and management. His experience as a student-athlete shaped his values, his work ethic, and his belief in the importance of mental health, leadership, and community.

Week 33
CALM UNDER PRESSURE

"You gain strength, courage, and confidence by every experience in which you really stop to look fear in the face."

— *Eleanor Roosevelt*

Athlete Insights: From Matt Brownlow.

"I use the 4-7-8 breathing technique to recenter and stay calm. It is okay to be nervous. It means you care."

Matt understands that nerves are not a weakness. They are a signal of investment. Instead of fighting anxiety, he uses intentional breathing to slow his thoughts and return to the present moment. This practice allows him to compete without distraction and access his full ability.

Conviction is trusting your preparation even when emotions rise. Calm does not come from the absence of pressure. It comes from knowing how to manage it.

Stay grounded by focusing on your breathing and remain calm by relying on your preparation.

Date ___/___/___

Rate each on a scale from 1-10 (1=low, 10=high)
 MOOD:___ STRESS:___ ENERGY:___ MOTIVATION:___

Am I satisfied with the work I did today to reach my goals?

☐ YES ☐ NO

If yes, what helped today?
If no, what can I refocus on tomorrow?

Date ___/___/___

Rate each on a scale from 1-10 (1=low, 10=high)
 MOOD:___ STRESS:___ ENERGY:___ MOTIVATION:___

Am I satisfied with the work I did today to reach my goals?

☐ YES ☐ NO

If yes, what helped today?
If no, what can I refocus on tomorrow?

Date ___/___/___

Rate each on a scale from 1-10 (1=low, 10=high)
 MOOD:___ STRESS:___ ENERGY:___ MOTIVATION:___

Am I satisfied with the work I did today to reach my goals?

☐ YES ☐ NO

If yes, what helped today?
If no, what can I refocus on tomorrow?

Date ___/___/___

Rate each on a scale from 1-10 (1=low, 10=high)

MOOD: ___ STRESS: ___ ENERGY: ___ MOTIVATION: ___

Am I satisfied with the work I did today to reach my goals?

☐ YES ☐ NO

If yes, what helped today?
If no, what can I refocus on tomorrow?

Date ___/___/___

Rate each on a scale from 1-10 (1=low, 10=high)

MOOD: ___ STRESS: ___ ENERGY: ___ MOTIVATION: ___

Am I satisfied with the work I did today to reach my goals?

☐ YES ☐ NO

If yes, what helped today?
If no, what can I refocus on tomorrow?

Date ___/___/___

Rate each on a scale from 1-10 (1=low, 10=high)

MOOD: ___ STRESS: ___ ENERGY: ___ MOTIVATION: ___

Am I satisfied with the work I did today to reach my goals?

☐ YES ☐ NO

If yes, what helped today?
If no, what can I refocus on tomorrow?

Date ___/___/___

Weekly Reflection

What emotion have I felt most often this week?

[ ]

Did I take time to notice how I was feeling before or after a big moment?

☐ YES ☐ NO

What was the moment? What did you notice. Whether or not you forgot to pay attention to how you were feeling at the time, how do you feel about it now?

[ ]

Write about a moment that challenged you mentally this week. How did you respond?

[ ]

How intense were your practices or workouts this week? Did anything shift mentally?

[ ]

Read Aloud:

I FOCUS ON WHAT I CAN CONTROL.
I AM PREPARED AND READY.

Week 34
UNDERSTANDING FEEDBACK

"Criticism, like rain, should be gentle enough to nourish a man's growth without destroying his roots."

— *Frank A. Clark*

Athlete Insights: From Matt Brownlow.

"Everyone offering feedback has your best interest. Different perspectives help you perfect your craft."

Matt approaches feedback with an open mind. He understands that coaches, teammates, and support staff all bring valuable perspectives shaped by experience. Conviction allows him to listen without ego and adjust without losing confidence.

This week is about separating identity from instruction. When your belief is strong, feedback becomes a tool instead of a threat.

Receive feedback as guidance, not judgment.

Date __/__/__

Rate each on a scale from 1-10 (1=low, 10=high)
MOOD:___ STRESS:___ ENERGY:___ MOTIVATION:___

Am I satisfied with the work I did today to reach my goals?

☐ YES ☐ NO

If yes, what helped today?
If no, what can I refocus on tomorrow?

Date __/__/__

Rate each on a scale from 1-10 (1=low, 10=high)
MOOD:___ STRESS:___ ENERGY:___ MOTIVATION:___

Am I satisfied with the work I did today to reach my goals?

☐ YES ☐ NO

If yes, what helped today?
If no, what can I refocus on tomorrow?

Date __/__/__

Rate each on a scale from 1-10 (1=low, 10=high)
MOOD:___ STRESS:___ ENERGY:___ MOTIVATION:___

Am I satisfied with the work I did today to reach my goals?

☐ YES ☐ NO

If yes, what helped today?
If no, what can I refocus on tomorrow?

Date ___/___/___

Rate each on a scale from 1-10 (1=low, 10=high)
 MOOD:___ STRESS:___ ENERGY:___ MOTIVATION:___

Am I satisfied with the work I did today to reach my goals?

☐ YES ☐ NO

If yes, what helped today?
If no, what can I refocus on tomorrow?

Date ___/___/___

Rate each on a scale from 1-10 (1=low, 10=high)
 MOOD:___ STRESS:___ ENERGY:___ MOTIVATION:___

Am I satisfied with the work I did today to reach my goals?

☐ YES ☐ NO

If yes, what helped today?
If no, what can I refocus on tomorrow?

Date ___/___/___

Rate each on a scale from 1-10 (1=low, 10=high)
 MOOD:___ STRESS:___ ENERGY:___ MOTIVATION:___

Am I satisfied with the work I did today to reach my goals?

☐ YES ☐ NO

If yes, what helped today?
If no, what can I refocus on tomorrow?

Date ___/___/___

Weekly Reflection

What emotion have I felt most often this week?

[ ]

Did I take time to notice how I was feeling before or after a big moment?

☐ YES   ☐ NO

What was the moment? What did you notice. Whether or not you forgot to pay attention to how you were feeling at the time, how do you feel about it now?

[ ]

Write about a moment that challenged you mentally this week. How did you respond?

[ ]

How intense were your practices or workouts this week? Did anything shift mentally?

[ ]

Read Aloud:

I FOCUS ON WHAT I CAN CONTROL.
I AM PREPARED AND READY.

Week 35
LEAN ON COMMUNITY

"Connection is why we are here."
- Brene Brown

Athlete Insights: From Matt Brownlow.

"Create and lean on your community. It is okay not to be okay. Ask for what you need."

Conviction does not mean doing everything alone. Matt learned that strength grows when you speak openly and lean on others. Community provides perspective, accountability, and support during uncertainty, injury, and transition.

This week is about recognizing that asking for help is not weakness. It is clarity. Conviction includes knowing when to reach out.

Strong conviction includes the courage to ask for support.

Date ___/___/___

Rate each on a scale from 1-10 (1=low, 10=high)
  MOOD:___ STRESS:___ ENERGY:___ MOTIVATION:___
Am I satisfied with the work I did today to reach my goals?

☐ YES ☐ NO

If yes, what helped today?
If no, what can I refocus on tomorrow?

Date ___/___/___

Rate each on a scale from 1-10 (1=low, 10=high)
  MOOD:___ STRESS:___ ENERGY:___ MOTIVATION:___
Am I satisfied with the work I did today to reach my goals?

☐ YES ☐ NO

If yes, what helped today?
If no, what can I refocus on tomorrow?

Date ___/___/___

Rate each on a scale from 1-10 (1=low, 10=high)
  MOOD:___ STRESS:___ ENERGY:___ MOTIVATION:___
Am I satisfied with the work I did today to reach my goals?

☐ YES ☐ NO

If yes, what helped today?
If no, what can I refocus on tomorrow?

Date ___/___/___

Rate each on a scale from 1-10 (1=low, 10=high)
  MOOD:___ STRESS:___ ENERGY:___ MOTIVATION:___

Am I satisfied with the work I did today to reach my goals?

  ☐ YES   ☐ NO

If yes, what helped today?
If no, what can I refocus on tomorrow?

Date ___/___/___

Rate each on a scale from 1-10 (1=low, 10=high)
  MOOD:___ STRESS:___ ENERGY:___ MOTIVATION:___

Am I satisfied with the work I did today to reach my goals?

  ☐ YES   ☐ NO

If yes, what helped today?
If no, what can I refocus on tomorrow?

Date ___/___/___

Rate each on a scale from 1-10 (1=low, 10=high)
  MOOD:___ STRESS:___ ENERGY:___ MOTIVATION:___

Am I satisfied with the work I did today to reach my goals?

  ☐ YES   ☐ NO

If yes, what helped today?
If no, what can I refocus on tomorrow?

Date ___/___/___

Weekly Reflection

What emotion have I felt most often this week?

[ ]

Did I take time to notice how I was feeling before or after a big moment?

☐ Yes ☐ No

What was the moment? What did you notice. Whether or not you forgot to pay attention to how you were feeling at the time, how do you feel about it now?

[ ]

Write about a moment that challenged you mentally this week. How did you respond?

[ ]

How intense were your practices or workouts this week? Did anything shift mentally?

[ ]

Read Aloud:

I FOCUS ON WHAT I CAN CONTROL.
I AM PREPARED AND READY.

Week 36
BELIEVE IN YOUR WORTH

"Believe you can and you are halfway there."
   - *Theodore Roosevelt*

Athlete Insights: From Matt Brownlow.

"When I am feeling low, I tell myself 'you have done good.' I remind myself that I am appreciated."

Matt practices conviction through gratitude and self-recognition. By acknowledging how far he has come, he reinforces belief in himself beyond performance. Saving positive messages and reminders helps him reconnect with his value during difficult moments.

Conviction is remembering your worth when doubt tries to speak louder than truth.

Honor your progress, journey, and committment, and remember to speak to yourself with respect.

Date ___/___/___

Rate each on a scale from 1-10 (1=low, 10=high)

MOOD: ___ STRESS: ___ ENERGY: ___ MOTIVATION: ___

Am I satisfied with the work I did today to reach my goals?

☐ YES   ☐ NO

If yes, what helped today?
If no, what can I refocus on tomorrow?

Date ___/___/___

Rate each on a scale from 1-10 (1=low, 10=high)

MOOD: ___ STRESS: ___ ENERGY: ___ MOTIVATION: ___

Am I satisfied with the work I did today to reach my goals?

☐ YES   ☐ NO

If yes, what helped today?
If no, what can I refocus on tomorrow?

Date ___/___/___

Rate each on a scale from 1-10 (1=low, 10=high)

MOOD: ___ STRESS: ___ ENERGY: ___ MOTIVATION: ___

Am I satisfied with the work I did today to reach my goals?

☐ YES   ☐ NO

If yes, what helped today?
If no, what can I refocus on tomorrow?

Date ___/___/___

Rate each on a scale from 1-10 (1=low, 10=high)
  MOOD:___ STRESS:___ ENERGY:___ MOTIVATION:___

Am I satisfied with the work I did today to reach my goals?

☐ YES   ☐ NO

If yes, what helped today?
If no, what can I refocus on tomorrow?

Date ___/___/___

Rate each on a scale from 1-10 (1=low, 10=high)
  MOOD:___ STRESS:___ ENERGY:___ MOTIVATION:___

Am I satisfied with the work I did today to reach my goals?

☐ YES   ☐ NO

If yes, what helped today?
If no, what can I refocus on tomorrow?

Date ___/___/___

Rate each on a scale from 1-10 (1=low, 10=high)
  MOOD:___ STRESS:___ ENERGY:___ MOTIVATION:___

Am I satisfied with the work I did today to reach my goals?

☐ YES   ☐ NO

If yes, what helped today?
If no, what can I refocus on tomorrow?

Date ___/___/___

Weekly Reflection

What emotion have I felt most often this week?

[ ]

Did I take time to notice how I was feeling before or after a big moment?

☐ YES   ☐ NO

What was the moment? What did you notice. Whether or not you forgot to pay attention to how you were feeling at the time, how do you feel about it now?

[ ]

Write about a moment that challenged you mentally this week. How did you respond?

[ ]

How intense were your practices or workouts this week? Did anything shift mentally?

[ ]

Read Aloud:

I FOCUS ON WHAT I CAN CONTROL.
I AM PREPARED AND READY.

MONTH 10
Discipline

What is Conviction?

Discipline isn't punishment or perfection. It's the choice to show up when it's hard. It's the quiet voice that says do it anyway. Discipline helps athletes stay consistent in chaos. It means choosing long-term goals over short-term moods, sticking to routines when motivation fades, and making decisions that align with your values even when no one's watching.

You don't have to be perfect to be disciplined. You just have to stay connected to your why and be willing to do the work even when you don't feel like it.

This month is about training that mindset and sharpening your focus on the little daily choices that create long-term success.

Meet the Athlete:

Jenna Ravenscroft

Jenna Ravenscraft is a coach, competitor, and all-around force of nature. Her athletic journey spans nearly every corner of the sports world.

She started Spartan racing in 2018 and wasted no time proving her toughness, completing a Trifecta that included a 4-hour, 12-hour, and ultra-distance challenge in the same year. In 2020, she and her team won the brutal Go Ruck Team Assessment, an event built to test physical and mental limits. In 2023 and 2024, she represented her team at the Hyrox World Championships in Nice, France.

Jenna doesn't just compete. She pushes others. She has coached college basketball at Treasure Valley Community College and worked with athletes in soccer, volleyball, basketball, and track. Her story reminds us that discipline isn't about being rigid. It's about being ready.

Week 37
THE POWER OF SHOWING UP

"Success is nothing more than a few simple disciplines practiced every day."
                                        - Jim Rohn

Athlete Insights: From Jenna Ravenscraft.

"Discipline is being able to show up for yourself when no one else is watching."

Jenna's story is a masterclass in internal motivation. She has competed across sports that test both physical stamina and mental grit, from college basketball to Spartan Ultra Races and world championship-level DEKA events. Her success has never come from hype or spotlight. It has come from discipline—the daily decision to show up, prepare, and grind through the hard moments.

This week, we focus on the power of consistency. Not perfection. Not hype. Just the quiet strength of being present, day after day, especially when no one is watching.

True discipline is not about feeling motivated. It is about honoring your values through your actions, even on the days you do not feel like it.

Date ___/___/___

Rate each on a scale from 1-10 (1=low, 10=high)

MOOD: ___ STRESS: ___ ENERGY: ___ MOTIVATION: ___

Am I satisfied with the work I did today to reach my goals?

☐ YES   ☐ NO

If yes, what helped today?
If no, what can I refocus on tomorrow?

Date ___/___/___

Rate each on a scale from 1-10 (1=low, 10=high)

MOOD: ___ STRESS: ___ ENERGY: ___ MOTIVATION: ___

Am I satisfied with the work I did today to reach my goals?

☐ YES   ☐ NO

If yes, what helped today?
If no, what can I refocus on tomorrow?

Date ___/___/___

Rate each on a scale from 1-10 (1=low, 10=high)

MOOD: ___ STRESS: ___ ENERGY: ___ MOTIVATION: ___

Am I satisfied with the work I did today to reach my goals?

☐ YES   ☐ NO

If yes, what helped today?
If no, what can I refocus on tomorrow?

Date __/__/__

Rate each on a scale from 1-10 (1=low, 10=high)
 MOOD: ___ STRESS: ___ ENERGY: ___ MOTIVATION: ___

Am I satisfied with the work I did today to reach my goals?

☐ YES ☐ NO

If yes, what helped today?
If no, what can I refocus on tomorrow?

Date __/__/__

Rate each on a scale from 1-10 (1=low, 10=high)
 MOOD: ___ STRESS: ___ ENERGY: ___ MOTIVATION: ___

Am I satisfied with the work I did today to reach my goals?

☐ YES ☐ NO

If yes, what helped today?
If no, what can I refocus on tomorrow?

Date __/__/__

Rate each on a scale from 1-10 (1=low, 10=high)
 MOOD: ___ STRESS: ___ ENERGY: ___ MOTIVATION: ___

Am I satisfied with the work I did today to reach my goals?

☐ YES ☐ NO

If yes, what helped today?
If no, what can I refocus on tomorrow?

Date ___/___/___

Weekly Reflection

What emotion have I felt most often this week?

[ ]

Did I take time to notice how I was feeling before or after a big moment?

☐ YES   ☐ NO

What was the moment? What did you notice. Whether or not you forgot to pay attention to how you were feeling at the time, how do you feel about it now?

[ ]

Write about a moment that challenged you mentally this week. How did you respond?

[ ]

How intense were your practices or workouts this week? Did anything shift mentally?

[ ]

Read Aloud:
I FOCUS ON WHAT I CAN CONTROL.
I AM PREPARED AND READY.

Week 38
PROGRESS OVER PERFECTION

"Small disciplines repeated with consistency every day lead to great achievements."
— *John C. Maxwell*

Athlete Insights: From Jenna Ravenscraft.

"Discipline doesn't mean you have to be perfect. It just means you keep going."

Jenna knows what it means to build strength brick by brick. Her athletic journey has spanned teams, solo races, championships, and setbacks. But the thing that kept her moving forward was not flawless performance. It was the discipline to keep showing up. To learn. To grow. And to keep climbing, even on days when progress felt small.

This week, we focus on giving consistent effort instead of chasing perfection. Whether you felt amazing or struggled, the fact that you are still showing up means you are building something powerful.

Discipline is not about doing it all perfectly. It is about sticking with the process, learning from mistakes, and staying committed to your goals.

Date ___/___/___

Rate each on a scale from 1-10 (1=low, 10=high)
 MOOD: ___ STRESS: ___ ENERGY: ___ MOTIVATION: ___

Am I satisfied with the work I did today to reach my goals?

☐ YES   ☐ No

If yes, what helped today?
If no, what can I refocus on tomorrow?

Date ___/___/___

Rate each on a scale from 1-10 (1=low, 10=high)
 MOOD: ___ STRESS: ___ ENERGY: ___ MOTIVATION: ___

Am I satisfied with the work I did today to reach my goals?

☐ YES   ☐ No

If yes, what helped today?
If no, what can I refocus on tomorrow?

Date ___/___/___

Rate each on a scale from 1-10 (1=low, 10=high)
 MOOD: ___ STRESS: ___ ENERGY: ___ MOTIVATION: ___

Am I satisfied with the work I did today to reach my goals?

☐ YES   ☐ No

If yes, what helped today?
If no, what can I refocus on tomorrow?

Date __/__/__

Rate each on a scale from 1-10 (1=low, 10=high)
 MOOD:___ STRESS:___ ENERGY:___ MOTIVATION:___
Am I satisfied with the work I did today to reach my goals?

☐ YES ☐ NO

If yes, what helped today?
If no, what can I refocus on tomorrow?

```
[                                                    ]
```

Date __/__/__

Rate each on a scale from 1-10 (1=low, 10=high)
 MOOD:___ STRESS:___ ENERGY:___ MOTIVATION:___
Am I satisfied with the work I did today to reach my goals?

☐ YES ☐ NO

If yes, what helped today?
If no, what can I refocus on tomorrow?

```
[                                                    ]
```

Date __/__/__

Rate each on a scale from 1-10 (1=low, 10=high)
 MOOD:___ STRESS:___ ENERGY:___ MOTIVATION:___
Am I satisfied with the work I did today to reach my goals?

☐ YES ☐ NO

If yes, what helped today?
If no, what can I refocus on tomorrow?

```
[                                                    ]
```

Date ___/___/___

Weekly Reflection

What emotion have I felt most often this week?

[ ]

Did I take time to notice how I was feeling before or after a big moment?

☐ YES ☐ NO

What was the moment? What did you notice. Whether or not you forgot to pay attention to how you were feeling at the time, how do you feel about it now?

[ ]

Write about a moment that challenged you mentally this week. How did you respond?

[ ]

How intense were your practices or workouts this week? Did anything shift mentally?

[ ]

Read Aloud:

I FOCUS ON WHAT I CAN CONTROL.
I AM PREPARED AND READY.

Week 39
DEVELOP DAILY HABITS

"Without self-discipline, success is impossible, period."

- Lou Holtz

Athlete Insights: From Jenna Ravenscraft.

"Life is all about adapting to what's next. I never want to be caught unprepared."

From the basketball court to the rugged terrain of Spartan races, Jenna has shown a remarkable ability to adjust her training, mindset, and performance to match the challenge in front of her. She doesn't define herself by a single sport or a single title. She pushes forward, constantly evolving, proving that conviction isn't about sticking to one thing, it's about showing up with intention no matter the arena.

Jenna's story reminds us that consistency isn't about repeating the same workout, strategy, or identity. It's about carrying your inner fire into whatever shape life demands.

Every obstacle can become an opportunity when I stay committed to growth, not comfort.

Date __/__/__

Rate each on a scale from 1-10 (1=low, 10=high)
 Mood:___ Stress:___ Energy:___ Motivation:___

Am I satisfied with the work I did today to reach my goals?

☐ Yes ☐ No

If yes, what helped today?
If no, what can I refocus on tomorrow?

Date __/__/__

Rate each on a scale from 1-10 (1=low, 10=high)
 Mood:___ Stress:___ Energy:___ Motivation:___

Am I satisfied with the work I did today to reach my goals?

☐ Yes ☐ No

If yes, what helped today?
If no, what can I refocus on tomorrow?

Date __/__/__

Rate each on a scale from 1-10 (1=low, 10=high)
 Mood:___ Stress:___ Energy:___ Motivation:___

Am I satisfied with the work I did today to reach my goals?

☐ Yes ☐ No

If yes, what helped today?
If no, what can I refocus on tomorrow?

Date ___/___/___

Rate each on a scale from 1-10 (1=low, 10=high)
MOOD:___ STRESS:___ ENERGY:___ MOTIVATION:___

Am I satisfied with the work I did today to reach my goals?

☐ YES ☐ NO

If yes, what helped today?
If no, what can I refocus on tomorrow?

Date ___/___/___

Rate each on a scale from 1-10 (1=low, 10=high)
MOOD:___ STRESS:___ ENERGY:___ MOTIVATION:___

Am I satisfied with the work I did today to reach my goals?

☐ YES ☐ NO

If yes, what helped today?
If no, what can I refocus on tomorrow?

Date ___/___/___

Rate each on a scale from 1-10 (1=low, 10=high)
MOOD:___ STRESS:___ ENERGY:___ MOTIVATION:___

Am I satisfied with the work I did today to reach my goals?

☐ YES ☐ NO

If yes, what helped today?
If no, what can I refocus on tomorrow?

Date ___/___/___

Weekly Reflection

What emotion have I felt most often this week?

```
[                                                    ]
```

Did I take time to notice how I was feeling before or after a big moment?

☐ YES　　　　　☐ No

What was the moment? What did you notice. Whether or not you forgot to pay attention to how you were feeling at the time, how do you feel about it now?

```
[                                                    ]
```

Write about a moment that challenged you mentally this week. How did you respond?

```
[                                                    ]
```

How intense were your practices or workouts this week? Did anything shift mentally?

```
[                                                    ]
```

Read Aloud:

I FOCUS ON WHAT I CAN CONTROL.
I AM PREPARED AND READY.

Week 40
STRENGTH IN STILLNESS

> *"Sometimes the most productive thing you can do is relax."*
>
> \- Mark Black

Athlete Insights: From Jenna Ravenscraft.

"Rest is part of the process. You have to let your body and mind recover if you want to perform at your best."

Jenna learned to respect recovery not as a luxury, but as a necessity. The grueling demands of endurance racing taught her that discipline includes knowing when to push and when to pause. Without time to reset, even the strongest competitors burn out.

This week is a reminder that stillness is not weakness. It is a weapon. Knowing when to rest, reflect, and recharge is a key part of long-term performance and personal growth.

Recovery is part of discipline. I don't earn strength by pushing nonstop, but by learning when to pause with purpose.

Date __/__/__

Rate each on a scale from 1-10 (1=low, 10=high)
 MOOD:___ STRESS:___ ENERGY:___ MOTIVATION:___
Am I satisfied with the work I did today to reach my goals?

☐ YES   ☐ NO

If yes, what helped today?
If no, what can I refocus on tomorrow?

Date __/__/__

Rate each on a scale from 1-10 (1=low, 10=high)
 MOOD:___ STRESS:___ ENERGY:___ MOTIVATION:___
Am I satisfied with the work I did today to reach my goals?

☐ YES   ☐ NO

If yes, what helped today?
If no, what can I refocus on tomorrow?

Date __/__/__

Rate each on a scale from 1-10 (1=low, 10=high)
 MOOD:___ STRESS:___ ENERGY:___ MOTIVATION:___
Am I satisfied with the work I did today to reach my goals?

☐ YES   ☐ NO

If yes, what helped today?
If no, what can I refocus on tomorrow?

Date ___/___/___

Rate each on a scale from 1-10 (1=low, 10=high)
 MOOD:___ STRESS:___ ENERGY:___ MOTIVATION:___

Am I satisfied with the work I did today to reach my goals?

☐ YES ☐ NO

If yes, what helped today?
If no, what can I refocus on tomorrow?

Date ___/___/___

Rate each on a scale from 1-10 (1=low, 10=high)
 MOOD:___ STRESS:___ ENERGY:___ MOTIVATION:___

Am I satisfied with the work I did today to reach my goals?

☐ YES ☐ NO

If yes, what helped today?
If no, what can I refocus on tomorrow?

Date ___/___/___

Rate each on a scale from 1-10 (1=low, 10=high)
 MOOD:___ STRESS:___ ENERGY:___ MOTIVATION:___

Am I satisfied with the work I did today to reach my goals?

☐ YES ☐ NO

If yes, what helped today?
If no, what can I refocus on tomorrow?

Date ___/___/___

Weekly Reflection

What emotion have I felt most often this week?

[ ]

Did I take time to notice how I was feeling before or after a big moment?

☐ YES   ☐ NO

What was the moment? What did you notice. Whether or not you forgot to pay attention to how you were feeling at the time, how do you feel about it now?

[ ]

Write about a moment that challenged you mentally this week. How did you respond?

[ ]

How intense were your practices or workouts this week? Did anything shift mentally?

[ ]

Read Aloud:

I FOCUS ON WHAT I CAN CONTROL.
I AM PREPARED AND READY.

MONTH 11
Self-Talk

What is Self-Talk?

Self-talk is the voice inside your mind that reacts to pressure, mistakes, success, and expectations. It shapes how you see yourself. It guides how you respond to stress. It influences confidence before you compete and resilience after you face challenges.

Positive self-talk is not about pretending everything is perfect. It is about choosing to speak to yourself with clarity, honesty, and belief. When you control your internal dialogue, you control your response to pressure, setbacks, and nerves.

This month, you will hear from JJ Dolan, a defensive back whose ability to steady himself through perspective and self-belief shows how powerful self-talk can be when the stakes are high.

Meet the Athlete:

JJ Dolan

JJ Dolan enters his sophomore season as a free safety and nickel cornerback at Montana State University. He earned First Team All-State and All-Conference honors as a nickel back at Missoula Sentinel High School, where he played on two state championship teams.

Known for his ability to stay composed and confident in high-pressure moments, JJ approaches the game with patience, perspective, and intentional self-talk.

Week 41
KEEP PERSPECTIVE

"Pressure is something you feel when you do not know what you are doing. Preparation prevents pressure."

— *Chuck Noll*

Athlete Insights: From JJ Dolan.

"I just remind myself that it is just a game. There is more to life than this competition."

JJ does not let the moment get bigger than it needs to be. When nerves show up before a game, he does not try to fight them. Instead, he steps back and remembers the bigger picture. This perspective helps him settle into the moment and play freely.

Pressure shrinks when perspective grows. By reminding himself that football is something he gets to do, not something he must be perfect at, JJ gives himself room to breathe, compete, and trust his preparation.

Stay grounded by remembering the bigger picture.

Date ___/___/___

Rate each on a scale from 1-10 (1=low, 10=high)
 MOOD:___ STRESS:___ ENERGY:___ MOTIVATION:___
Am I satisfied with the work I did today to reach my goals?

☐ YES   ☐ NO

If yes, what helped today?
If no, what can I refocus on tomorrow?

Date ___/___/___

Rate each on a scale from 1-10 (1=low, 10=high)
 MOOD:___ STRESS:___ ENERGY:___ MOTIVATION:___
Am I satisfied with the work I did today to reach my goals?

☐ YES   ☐ NO

If yes, what helped today?
If no, what can I refocus on tomorrow?

Date ___/___/___

Rate each on a scale from 1-10 (1=low, 10=high)
 MOOD:___ STRESS:___ ENERGY:___ MOTIVATION:___
Am I satisfied with the work I did today to reach my goals?

☐ YES   ☐ NO

If yes, what helped today?
If no, what can I refocus on tomorrow?

Date ___/___/___

Rate each on a scale from 1-10 (1=low, 10=high)
  MOOD:___ STRESS:___ ENERGY:___ MOTIVATION:___

Am I satisfied with the work I did today to reach my goals?

  ☐ YES   ☐ NO

If yes, what helped today?
If no, what can I refocus on tomorrow?

Date ___/___/___

Rate each on a scale from 1-10 (1=low, 10=high)
  MOOD:___ STRESS:___ ENERGY:___ MOTIVATION:___

Am I satisfied with the work I did today to reach my goals?

  ☐ YES   ☐ NO

If yes, what helped today?
If no, what can I refocus on tomorrow?

Date ___/___/___

Rate each on a scale from 1-10 (1=low, 10=high)
  MOOD:___ STRESS:___ ENERGY:___ MOTIVATION:___

Am I satisfied with the work I did today to reach my goals?

  ☐ YES   ☐ NO

If yes, what helped today?
If no, what can I refocus on tomorrow?

Date ___/___/___

Weekly Reflection

What emotion have I felt most often this week?

[ ]

Did I take time to notice how I was feeling before or after a big moment?

☐ YES ☐ NO

What was the moment? What did you notice. Whether or not you forgot to pay attention to how you were feeling at the time, how do you feel about it now?

[ ]

Write about a moment that challenged you mentally this week. How did you respond?

[ ]

How intense were your practices or workouts this week? Did anything shift mentally?

[ ]

Read Aloud:

I FOCUS ON WHAT I CAN CONTROL.
I AM PREPARED AND READY.

Week 42
LEARN FROM MISTAKES

"Failure is not fatal. But failure to change might be."

— *John Wooden*

Athlete Insights: From JJ Dolan.

"I think about everything I did wrong in the loss so in the future I will not make the same mistake."

Self-talk is not just encouragement. It is also honest reflection. JJ studies mistakes so he can grow. The goal is not to dwell or criticize. The goal is to learn. Instead of letting setbacks shake his confidence, he turns them into direction.

This week is about using mistakes as teachers. Reflection builds improvement. Self-talk shapes how you respond to frustration. Growth begins when you look at your performance without fear.

Mistakes are information. Use them.

Date ___/___/___

Rate each on a scale from 1-10 (1=low, 10=high)
 MOOD:___ STRESS:___ ENERGY:___ MOTIVATION:___

Am I satisfied with the work I did today to reach my goals?

☐ YES   ☐ NO

If yes, what helped today?
If no, what can I refocus on tomorrow?

Date ___/___/___

Rate each on a scale from 1-10 (1=low, 10=high)
 MOOD:___ STRESS:___ ENERGY:___ MOTIVATION:___

Am I satisfied with the work I did today to reach my goals?

☐ YES   ☐ NO

If yes, what helped today?
If no, what can I refocus on tomorrow?

Date ___/___/___

Rate each on a scale from 1-10 (1=low, 10=high)
 MOOD:___ STRESS:___ ENERGY:___ MOTIVATION:___

Am I satisfied with the work I did today to reach my goals?

☐ YES   ☐ NO

If yes, what helped today?
If no, what can I refocus on tomorrow?

Date ___/___/___

Rate each on a scale from 1-10 (1=low, 10=high)
 MOOD:___ STRESS:___ ENERGY:___ MOTIVATION:___

Am I satisfied with the work I did today to reach my goals?

☐ YES ☐ NO

If yes, what helped today?
If no, what can I refocus on tomorrow?

Date ___/___/___

Rate each on a scale from 1-10 (1=low, 10=high)
 MOOD:___ STRESS:___ ENERGY:___ MOTIVATION:___

Am I satisfied with the work I did today to reach my goals?

☐ YES ☐ NO

If yes, what helped today?
If no, what can I refocus on tomorrow?

Date ___/___/___

Rate each on a scale from 1-10 (1=low, 10=high)
 MOOD:___ STRESS:___ ENERGY:___ MOTIVATION:___

Am I satisfied with the work I did today to reach my goals?

☐ YES ☐ NO

If yes, what helped today?
If no, what can I refocus on tomorrow?

Date ___/___/___

Weekly Reflection

What emotion have I felt most often this week?

[ ]

Did I take time to notice how I was feeling before or after a big moment?

☐ YES   ☐ NO

What was the moment? What did you notice. Whether or not you forgot to pay attention to how you were feeling at the time, how do you feel about it now?

[ ]

Write about a moment that challenged you mentally this week. How did you respond?

[ ]

How intense were your practices or workouts this week? Did anything shift mentally?

[ ]

Read Aloud:
I FOCUS ON WHAT I CAN CONTROL.
I AM PREPARED AND READY.

Week 43
TRUST IN COACHING

"Coaching is unlocking a person's potential to maximize their performance."
- John Whitmore

Athlete Insights: From JJ Dolan.

"Coaches are going to coach you hard because they want you to reach your goals."

For many of us, feedback can feel personal in competitive environments. JJ keeps himself grounded by remembering that intensity from coaches comes from belief and expectation. He does not let correction become criticism in his mind.

When you trust that feedback is support, not judgment, your self-talk shifts from defense to development. The goal of coaching is growth, not perfection. Let instruction strengthen your confidence instead of challenging it.

View feedback as belief in your potential.

Date ___/___/___

Rate each on a scale from 1-10 (1=low, 10=high)
 MOOD:___ STRESS:___ ENERGY:___ MOTIVATION:___

Am I satisfied with the work I did today to reach my goals?

☐ YES ☐ NO

If yes, what helped today?
If no, what can I refocus on tomorrow?

Date ___/___/___

Rate each on a scale from 1-10 (1=low, 10=high)
 MOOD:___ STRESS:___ ENERGY:___ MOTIVATION:___

Am I satisfied with the work I did today to reach my goals?

☐ YES ☐ NO

If yes, what helped today?
If no, what can I refocus on tomorrow?

Date ___/___/___

Rate each on a scale from 1-10 (1=low, 10=high)
 MOOD:___ STRESS:___ ENERGY:___ MOTIVATION:___

Am I satisfied with the work I did today to reach my goals?

☐ YES ☐ NO

If yes, what helped today?
If no, what can I refocus on tomorrow?

Date __/__/__

Rate each on a scale from 1-10 (1=low, 10=high)
MOOD:___ STRESS:___ ENERGY:___ MOTIVATION:___

Am I satisfied with the work I did today to reach my goals?

☐ YES ☐ NO

If yes, what helped today?
If no, what can I refocus on tomorrow?

Date __/__/__

Rate each on a scale from 1-10 (1=low, 10=high)
MOOD:___ STRESS:___ ENERGY:___ MOTIVATION:___

Am I satisfied with the work I did today to reach my goals?

☐ YES ☐ NO

If yes, what helped today?
If no, what can I refocus on tomorrow?

Date __/__/__

Rate each on a scale from 1-10 (1=low, 10=high)
MOOD:___ STRESS:___ ENERGY:___ MOTIVATION:___

Am I satisfied with the work I did today to reach my goals?

☐ YES ☐ NO

If yes, what helped today?
If no, what can I refocus on tomorrow?

Date __/__/__

Weekly Reflection

What emotion have I felt most often this week?

[ ]

Did I take time to notice how I was feeling before or after a big moment?

☐ YES   ☐ NO

What was the moment? What did you notice. Whether or not you forgot to pay attention to how you were feeling at the time, how do you feel about it now?

[ ]

Write about a moment that challenged you mentally this week. How did you respond?

[ ]

How intense were your practices or workouts this week? Did anything shift mentally?

[ ]

Read Aloud:

I FOCUS ON WHAT I CAN CONTROL.
I AM PREPARED AND READY.

Week 44
CONFIDENCE IN YOUR PATH

"No one is you, and that is your power."
- Dave Grohl

Athlete Insights: From JJ Dolan.

"I tell myself God put me here for a reason and I am just as good or better than anyone in the room."

JJ's confidence comes from knowing he belongs. He does not compare himself to teammates or opponents. Instead, he anchors himself in purpose and preparation. When self-talk centers on belonging, performance becomes less about proving and more about playing.

This week is about speaking to yourself with belief. Confidence is built from your work, your identity, and your purpose. Trust that you are where you are meant to be.

Belonging begins when you believe you belong.

Date ___/___/___

Rate each on a scale from 1-10 (1=low, 10=high)
 MOOD:___ STRESS:___ ENERGY:___ MOTIVATION:___
Am I satisfied with the work I did today to reach my goals?

☐ YES ☐ NO

If yes, what helped today?
If no, what can I refocus on tomorrow?

Date ___/___/___

Rate each on a scale from 1-10 (1=low, 10=high)
 MOOD:___ STRESS:___ ENERGY:___ MOTIVATION:___
Am I satisfied with the work I did today to reach my goals?

☐ YES ☐ NO

If yes, what helped today?
If no, what can I refocus on tomorrow?

Date ___/___/___

Rate each on a scale from 1-10 (1=low, 10=high)
 MOOD:___ STRESS:___ ENERGY:___ MOTIVATION:___
Am I satisfied with the work I did today to reach my goals?

☐ YES ☐ NO

If yes, what helped today?
If no, what can I refocus on tomorrow?

Date __/__/__

Rate each on a scale from 1-10 (1=low, 10=high)
  MOOD:___ STRESS:___ ENERGY:___ MOTIVATION:___

Am I satisfied with the work I did today to reach my goals?

☐ YES   ☐ NO

If yes, what helped today?
If no, what can I refocus on tomorrow?

```
[                                                    ]
```

Date __/__/__

Rate each on a scale from 1-10 (1=low, 10=high)
  MOOD:___ STRESS:___ ENERGY:___ MOTIVATION:___

Am I satisfied with the work I did today to reach my goals?

☐ YES   ☐ NO

If yes, what helped today?
If no, what can I refocus on tomorrow?

```
[                                                    ]
```

Date __/__/__

Rate each on a scale from 1-10 (1=low, 10=high)
  MOOD:___ STRESS:___ ENERGY:___ MOTIVATION:___

Am I satisfied with the work I did today to reach my goals?

☐ YES   ☐ NO

If yes, what helped today?
If no, what can I refocus on tomorrow?

```
[                                                    ]
```

Date ___/___/___

Weekly Reflection

What emotion have I felt most often this week?

[ ]

Did I take time to notice how I was feeling before or after a big moment?

☐ YES   ☐ NO

What was the moment? What did you notice. Whether or not you forgot to pay attention to how you were feeling at the time, how do you feel about it now?

[ ]

Write about a moment that challenged you mentally this week. How did you respond?

[ ]

How intense were your practices or workouts this week? Did anything shift mentally?

[ ]

Read Aloud:

I FOCUS ON WHAT I CAN CONTROL.
I AM PREPARED AND READY.

MONTH 12
Perspective

What is Perspective?

Perspective is the ability to step back and look at the bigger picture. It is the understanding that every moment in your athletic journey is part of something larger. Perspective helps you stay calm under pressure, learn from mistakes without dwelling on them, and value the people and experiences around you.

Athletes with perspective compete with clarity. They remember why they play and who they play for. They understand that setbacks are temporary, improvement is ongoing, and identity is bigger than performance. Perspective keeps you grounded when emotions rise and keeps you steady when expectations feel heavy.

This month, you will learn from Cohen Groener, who has built his athletic mindset on preparation, understanding, patience, and the ability to zoom out when things feel intense.

Meet the Athlete:

Cohen Groener

Cohen Groener grew up in Billings, Montana, competing in multiple sports throughout his childhood and high school years. At Billings West, he was a two-sport athlete in football and basketball, and he earned a roster spot in the Montana East/West Shrine Game before continuing his career as a cornerback at Rocky Mountain College.

Cohen's mindset is shaped by balance, thoughtful reflection, and respect for the game. He understands the importance of preparation, letting go of frustration, listening for meaning, and staying aligned with his own path.

Week 45
STEADY IN THE MOMENT

"Calmness is the cradle of power."
- Josiah Glibert Holland

Athlete Insights: From Cohen Groener.

"I handle pressure with calming music and trusting that I prepared the best I could."

Perspective helps you stay grounded when emotions rise. Cohen does not try to eliminate nerves. He simply reminds himself that he has already done the work. When you trust your preparation, the moment becomes manageable. Pressure loses its weight.

This week is about recognizing that you play best when you are settled. Let your preparation support you. Let your breathing guide you. Let calmness give you clarity.

Trust the work. Let your mind settle into the moment.

Date __/__/__

Rate each on a scale from 1-10 (1=low, 10=high)
 MOOD:___ STRESS:___ ENERGY:___ MOTIVATION:___

Am I satisfied with the work I did today to reach my goals?

☐ YES ☐ NO

If yes, what helped today?
If no, what can I refocus on tomorrow?

Date __/__/__

Rate each on a scale from 1-10 (1=low, 10=high)
 MOOD:___ STRESS:___ ENERGY:___ MOTIVATION:___

Am I satisfied with the work I did today to reach my goals?

☐ YES ☐ NO

If yes, what helped today?
If no, what can I refocus on tomorrow?

Date __/__/__

Rate each on a scale from 1-10 (1=low, 10=high)
 MOOD:___ STRESS:___ ENERGY:___ MOTIVATION:___

Am I satisfied with the work I did today to reach my goals?

☐ YES ☐ NO

If yes, what helped today?
If no, what can I refocus on tomorrow?

Date ___/___/___

Rate each on a scale from 1-10 (1=low, 10=high)
  MOOD:___ STRESS:___ ENERGY:___ MOTIVATION:___
Am I satisfied with the work I did today to reach my goals?

☐ YES ☐ NO

If yes, what helped today?
If no, what can I refocus on tomorrow?

Date ___/___/___

Rate each on a scale from 1-10 (1=low, 10=high)
  MOOD:___ STRESS:___ ENERGY:___ MOTIVATION:___
Am I satisfied with the work I did today to reach my goals?

☐ YES ☐ NO

If yes, what helped today?
If no, what can I refocus on tomorrow?

Date ___/___/___

Rate each on a scale from 1-10 (1=low, 10=high)
  MOOD:___ STRESS:___ ENERGY:___ MOTIVATION:___
Am I satisfied with the work I did today to reach my goals?

☐ YES ☐ NO

If yes, what helped today?
If no, what can I refocus on tomorrow?

Date ___/___/___

Weekly Reflection

What emotion have I felt most often this week?

[ ]

Did I take time to notice how I was feeling before or after a big moment?

☐ YES ☐ NO

What was the moment? What did you notice. Whether or not you forgot to pay attention to how you were feeling at the time, how do you feel about it now?

[ ]

Write about a moment that challenged you mentally this week. How did you respond?

[ ]

How intense were your practices or workouts this week? Did anything shift mentally?

[ ]

Read Aloud:

I FOCUS ON WHAT I CAN CONTROL.
I AM PREPARED AND READY.

Week 46
FEEL IT, THEN RELEASE IT

"Emotions are meant to be felt, not lived in forever."

- Unknown

Athlete Insights: From Cohen Groener.

"I use the 24-hour rule. I allow myself to feel frustration, then I move on to the next goal."

Perspective does not ignore emotions. It makes room for them. Cohen knows that reflection has a time and place. He allows himself to process disappointment, but he does not stay stuck in it. This balance prevents setbacks from becoming long-term distractions.

This week is about honoring your feelings without letting them control your future.

Experience the moment, then release it and continue forward.

Date ___/___/___

Rate each on a scale from 1-10 (1=low, 10=high)
  MOOD: ___ STRESS: ___ ENERGY: ___ MOTIVATION: ___

Am I satisfied with the work I did today to reach my goals?

☐ YES   ☐ NO

If yes, what helped today?
If no, what can I refocus on tomorrow?

Date ___/___/___

Rate each on a scale from 1-10 (1=low, 10=high)
  MOOD: ___ STRESS: ___ ENERGY: ___ MOTIVATION: ___

Am I satisfied with the work I did today to reach my goals?

☐ YES   ☐ NO

If yes, what helped today?
If no, what can I refocus on tomorrow?

Date ___/___/___

Rate each on a scale from 1-10 (1=low, 10=high)
  MOOD: ___ STRESS: ___ ENERGY: ___ MOTIVATION: ___

Am I satisfied with the work I did today to reach my goals?

☐ YES   ☐ NO

If yes, what helped today?
If no, what can I refocus on tomorrow?

Date ___/___/___

Rate each on a scale from 1-10 (1=low, 10=high)

MOOD: ___ STRESS: ___ ENERGY: ___ MOTIVATION: ___

Am I satisfied with the work I did today to reach my goals?

☐ YES ☐ NO

If yes, what helped today?
If no, what can I refocus on tomorrow?

Date ___/___/___

Rate each on a scale from 1-10 (1=low, 10=high)

MOOD: ___ STRESS: ___ ENERGY: ___ MOTIVATION: ___

Am I satisfied with the work I did today to reach my goals?

☐ YES ☐ NO

If yes, what helped today?
If no, what can I refocus on tomorrow?

Date ___/___/___

Rate each on a scale from 1-10 (1=low, 10=high)

MOOD: ___ STRESS: ___ ENERGY: ___ MOTIVATION: ___

Am I satisfied with the work I did today to reach my goals?

☐ YES ☐ NO

If yes, what helped today?
If no, what can I refocus on tomorrow?

Date ___/___/___

Weekly Reflection

What emotion have I felt most often this week?

[ ]

Did I take time to notice how I was feeling before or after a big moment?

☐ YES   ☐ NO

What was the moment? What did you notice. Whether or not you forgot to pay attention to how you were feeling at the time, how do you feel about it now?

[ ]

Write about a moment that challenged you mentally this week. How did you respond?

[ ]

How intense were your practices or workouts this week? Did anything shift mentally?

[ ]

Read Aloud:

I FOCUS ON WHAT I CAN CONTROL.
I AM PREPARED AND READY.

Week 47
LISTEN FOR THE MESSAGE

"Most people do not listen to understand. They listen to reply."
- *Stephen R. Covey*

Athlete Insights: From Cohen Groener.

"I listen to what coaches say, not how they say it."

Emotion can distort communication. Perspective helps you filter information more clearly. Cohen understands that intensity from a coach often comes from passion, not frustration. By focusing on the meaning, not the tone, he grows instead of reacting.

This week is about responding instead of reacting. Slowing down. Listening for direction. Letting feedback be fuel.

Receive feedback with openness, not defensiveness.

Date ___/___/___

Rate each on a scale from 1-10 (1=low, 10=high)
 MOOD: ___ STRESS: ___ ENERGY: ___ MOTIVATION: ___

Am I satisfied with the work I did today to reach my goals?

☐ YES   ☐ NO

If yes, what helped today?
If no, what can I refocus on tomorrow?

Date ___/___/___

Rate each on a scale from 1-10 (1=low, 10=high)
 MOOD: ___ STRESS: ___ ENERGY: ___ MOTIVATION: ___

Am I satisfied with the work I did today to reach my goals?

☐ YES   ☐ NO

If yes, what helped today?
If no, what can I refocus on tomorrow?

Date ___/___/___

Rate each on a scale from 1-10 (1=low, 10=high)
 MOOD: ___ STRESS: ___ ENERGY: ___ MOTIVATION: ___

Am I satisfied with the work I did today to reach my goals?

☐ YES   ☐ NO

If yes, what helped today?
If no, what can I refocus on tomorrow?

Date ___/___/___

Rate each on a scale from 1-10 (1=low, 10=high)
 MOOD: ___ STRESS: ___ ENERGY: ___ MOTIVATION: ___

Am I satisfied with the work I did today to reach my goals?

☐ YES   ☐ NO

If yes, what helped today?
If no, what can I refocus on tomorrow?

Date ___/___/___

Rate each on a scale from 1-10 (1=low, 10=high)
 MOOD: ___ STRESS: ___ ENERGY: ___ MOTIVATION: ___

Am I satisfied with the work I did today to reach my goals?

☐ YES   ☐ NO

If yes, what helped today?
If no, what can I refocus on tomorrow?

Date ___/___/___

Rate each on a scale from 1-10 (1=low, 10=high)
 MOOD: ___ STRESS: ___ ENERGY: ___ MOTIVATION: ___

Am I satisfied with the work I did today to reach my goals?

☐ YES   ☐ NO

If yes, what helped today?
If no, what can I refocus on tomorrow?

Date ___/___/___

Weekly Reflection

What emotion have I felt most often this week?

```
┌─────────────────────────────────────────────┐
│                                             │
│                                             │
└─────────────────────────────────────────────┘
```

Did I take time to notice how I was feeling before or after a big moment?

☐ YES   ☐ NO

What was the moment? What did you notice. Whether or not you forgot to pay attention to how you were feeling at the time, how do you feel about it now?

```
┌─────────────────────────────────────────────┐
│                                             │
│                                             │
│                                             │
│                                             │
└─────────────────────────────────────────────┘
```

Write about a moment that challenged you mentally this week. How did you respond?

```
┌─────────────────────────────────────────────┐
│                                             │
│                                             │
│                                             │
│                                             │
└─────────────────────────────────────────────┘
```

How intense were your practices or workouts this week? Did anything shift mentally?

```
┌─────────────────────────────────────────────┐
│                                             │
│                                             │
│                                             │
│                                             │
└─────────────────────────────────────────────┘
```

Read Aloud:

I FOCUS ON WHAT I CAN CONTROL.
I AM PREPARED AND READY.

Week 48
FOLLOW YOUR OWN PATH

"Comparison is the thief of joy."
- *Theodore Roosevelt*

Athlete Insights: From Cohen Groener.

"It is me vs me. I can only control what I can control."

Perspective allows you to measure success by your own growth. Cohen reminds himself daily that comparison has no value in performance. The only meaningful competition is with the person you were yesterday.

This week is about recognizing your growth, your habits, your improvement. Your timeline is yours, no one else's.

Progress is personal. Honor your own journey.

Date ___/___/___

Rate each on a scale from 1-10 (1=low, 10=high)

MOOD: ___ STRESS: ___ ENERGY: ___ MOTIVATION: ___

Am I satisfied with the work I did today to reach my goals?

☐ YES ☐ NO

If yes, what helped today?
If no, what can I refocus on tomorrow?

Date ___/___/___

Rate each on a scale from 1-10 (1=low, 10=high)

MOOD: ___ STRESS: ___ ENERGY: ___ MOTIVATION: ___

Am I satisfied with the work I did today to reach my goals?

☐ YES ☐ NO

If yes, what helped today?
If no, what can I refocus on tomorrow?

Date ___/___/___

Rate each on a scale from 1-10 (1=low, 10=high)

MOOD: ___ STRESS: ___ ENERGY: ___ MOTIVATION: ___

Am I satisfied with the work I did today to reach my goals?

☐ YES ☐ NO

If yes, what helped today?
If no, what can I refocus on tomorrow?

Date ___/___/___

Rate each on a scale from 1-10 (1=low, 10=high)
 MOOD: ___ STRESS: ___ ENERGY: ___ MOTIVATION: ___
Am I satisfied with the work I did today to reach my goals?

☐ YES   ☐ NO

If yes, what helped today?
If no, what can I refocus on tomorrow?

Date ___/___/___

Rate each on a scale from 1-10 (1=low, 10=high)
 MOOD: ___ STRESS: ___ ENERGY: ___ MOTIVATION: ___
Am I satisfied with the work I did today to reach my goals?

☐ YES   ☐ NO

If yes, what helped today?
If no, what can I refocus on tomorrow?

Date ___/___/___

Rate each on a scale from 1-10 (1=low, 10=high)
 MOOD: ___ STRESS: ___ ENERGY: ___ MOTIVATION: ___
Am I satisfied with the work I did today to reach my goals?

☐ YES   ☐ NO

If yes, what helped today?
If no, what can I refocus on tomorrow?

Date ___/___/___

Weekly Reflection

What emotion have I felt most often this week?

```
┌─────────────────────────────────────────────┐
│                                             │
│                                             │
└─────────────────────────────────────────────┘
```

Did I take time to notice how I was feeling before or after a big moment?

☐ YES   ☐ NO

What was the moment? What did you notice. Whether or not you forgot to pay attention to how you were feeling at the time, how do you feel about it now?

```
┌─────────────────────────────────────────────┐
│                                             │
│                                             │
│                                             │
│                                             │
└─────────────────────────────────────────────┘
```

Write about a moment that challenged you mentally this week. How did you respond?

```
┌─────────────────────────────────────────────┐
│                                             │
│                                             │
│                                             │
│                                             │
└─────────────────────────────────────────────┘
```

How intense were your practices or workouts this week? Did anything shift mentally?

```
┌─────────────────────────────────────────────┐
│                                             │
│                                             │
│                                             │
│                                             │
└─────────────────────────────────────────────┘
```

Read Aloud:

I FOCUS ON WHAT I CAN CONTROL.
I AM PREPARED AND READY.

YEAR END
Reflection

What is Reflection?

Reflection is the act of looking back with intention. It gives meaning to the work you have done, the challenges you faced, and the progress you made. It allows you to recognize your growth and decide how you want to move forward.

This chapter is not about judging your journey.
It is about understanding it.

Your goal is to notice:

What changed within you
What mattered most
How your mindset evolved
Who you are becoming
Take your time. Be honest. This is your space.

You've spent nearly a whole year showing up.

THE LAST SECTION IS ABOUT MAKING THE MOST SENSE OUT OF YOUR JOURNEY!

Week 49
LOOKING BACK

"Reflection is one of the most underused yet powerful tools for success."
— *Richard Carlson*

This week is about perspective.

You do not need perfect memory or detailed notes. You only need honesty. Look back on the year as a whole. Notice the highs, the lows, the moments that felt important, and the ones that quietly shaped you.

Growth is not always loud. Sometimes it shows up in how you handle pressure, how you respond to setbacks, or how you talk to yourself when things do not go your way.

This week is not about judging your performance. It is about noticing it.

Date ___/___/___

Rate each on a scale from 1-10 (1=low, 10=high)

Mood: ___ Stress: ___ Energy: ___ Motivation: ___

Am I satisfied with the work I did today to reach my goals?

☐ Yes   ☐ No

If yes, what helped today?
If no, what can I refocus on tomorrow?

```
┌─────────────────────────────────────────┐
│                                         │
│                                         │
│                                         │
└─────────────────────────────────────────┘
```

Date ___/___/___

Rate each on a scale from 1-10 (1=low, 10=high)

Mood: ___ Stress: ___ Energy: ___ Motivation: ___

Am I satisfied with the work I did today to reach my goals?

☐ Yes   ☐ No

If yes, what helped today?
If no, what can I refocus on tomorrow?

```
┌─────────────────────────────────────────┐
│                                         │
│                                         │
│                                         │
└─────────────────────────────────────────┘
```

Date ___/___/___

Rate each on a scale from 1-10 (1=low, 10=high)

Mood: ___ Stress: ___ Energy: ___ Motivation: ___

Am I satisfied with the work I did today to reach my goals?

☐ Yes   ☐ No

If yes, what helped today?
If no, what can I refocus on tomorrow?

```
┌─────────────────────────────────────────┐
│                                         │
│                                         │
│                                         │
└─────────────────────────────────────────┘
```

Date ___/___/___

Rate each on a scale from 1-10 (1=low, 10=high)
MOOD:___ STRESS:___ ENERGY:___ MOTIVATION:___

Am I satisfied with the work I did today to reach my goals?

☐ YES   ☐ NO

If yes, what helped today?
If no, what can I refocus on tomorrow?

Date ___/___/___

Rate each on a scale from 1-10 (1=low, 10=high)
MOOD:___ STRESS:___ ENERGY:___ MOTIVATION:___

Am I satisfied with the work I did today to reach my goals?

☐ YES   ☐ NO

If yes, what helped today?
If no, what can I refocus on tomorrow?

Date ___/___/___

Rate each on a scale from 1-10 (1=low, 10=high)
MOOD:___ STRESS:___ ENERGY:___ MOTIVATION:___

Am I satisfied with the work I did today to reach my goals?

☐ YES   ☐ NO

If yes, what helped today?
If no, what can I refocus on tomorrow?

Date ___/___/___

Weekly Reflection

What emotion have I felt most often this week?

[ ]

Did I take time to notice how I was feeling before or after a big moment?

☐ YES   ☐ NO

What was the moment? What did you notice. Whether or not you forgot to pay attention to how you were feeling at the time, how do you feel about it now?

[ ]

Write about a moment that challenged you mentally this week. How did you respond?

[ ]

How intense were your practices or workouts this week? Did anything shift mentally?

[ ]

Read Aloud:

**I FOCUS ON WHAT I CAN CONTROL.
I AM PREPARED AND READY.**

Week 50
THE MENTAL GAME

"What you think determines how you feel, and how you feel determines how you act."
— *Rick Hanson*

This journal was never just about wins, losses, or stats. It was about how you think, reset, and respond.

The mental game shows up when things are hard. When motivation fades. When pressure builds. When nobody is watching.

This week, reflect on how your mindset has changed. Not how you wish it had changed, but how it actually has.

Awareness. Focus. Resilience. Confidence. Discipline. These are no longer concepts. They are skills you have practiced.

Date __/__/__

Rate each on a scale from 1-10 (1=low, 10=high)
 MOOD: ___ STRESS: ___ ENERGY: ___ MOTIVATION: ___
Am I satisfied with the work I did today to reach my goals?

☐ YES ☐ NO

If yes, what helped today?
If no, what can I refocus on tomorrow?

Date __/__/__

Rate each on a scale from 1-10 (1=low, 10=high)
 MOOD: ___ STRESS: ___ ENERGY: ___ MOTIVATION: ___
Am I satisfied with the work I did today to reach my goals?

☐ YES ☐ NO

If yes, what helped today?
If no, what can I refocus on tomorrow?

Date __/__/__

Rate each on a scale from 1-10 (1=low, 10=high)
 MOOD: ___ STRESS: ___ ENERGY: ___ MOTIVATION: ___
Am I satisfied with the work I did today to reach my goals?

☐ YES ☐ NO

If yes, what helped today?
If no, what can I refocus on tomorrow?

Date __/__/__

Rate each on a scale from 1-10 (1=low, 10=high)

MOOD: ___ STRESS: ___ ENERGY: ___ MOTIVATION: ___

Am I satisfied with the work I did today to reach my goals?

☐ YES   ☐ NO

If yes, what helped today?
If no, what can I refocus on tomorrow?

Date __/__/__

Rate each on a scale from 1-10 (1=low, 10=high)

MOOD: ___ STRESS: ___ ENERGY: ___ MOTIVATION: ___

Am I satisfied with the work I did today to reach my goals?

☐ YES   ☐ NO

If yes, what helped today?
If no, what can I refocus on tomorrow?

Date __/__/__

Rate each on a scale from 1-10 (1=low, 10=high)

MOOD: ___ STRESS: ___ ENERGY: ___ MOTIVATION: ___

Am I satisfied with the work I did today to reach my goals?

☐ YES   ☐ NO

If yes, what helped today?
If no, what can I refocus on tomorrow?

Date ___/___/___

Weekly Reflection

What emotion have I felt most often this week?

```
[                                                    ]
```

Did I take time to notice how I was feeling before or after a big moment?

☐ YES   ☐ NO

What was the moment? What did you notice. Whether or not you forgot to pay attention to how you were feeling at the time, how do you feel about it now?

```
[                                                    ]
```

Write about a moment that challenged you mentally this week. How did you respond?

```
[                                                    ]
```

How intense were your practices or workouts this week? Did anything shift mentally?

```
[                                                    ]
```

Read Aloud:

I FOCUS ON WHAT I CAN CONTROL.
I AM PREPARED AND READY.

IDENTITY AND PURPOSE

"You are more than the role you play."
— *Esther Perel*

Sport is something you do.

It is not all of who you are.

Over this year, you have learned things that go beyond competition. Lessons about effort, accountability, leadership, and resilience. Those lessons do not disappear when the season ends.

This week is about identity.

Who you are when you are competing.

Who you are when you are not.

The strongest athletes know themselves outside the game. That clarity builds confidence, balance, and purpose.

Date ___/___/___

Rate each on a scale from 1-10 (1=low, 10=high)
 Mood:___ Stress:___ Energy:___ Motivation:___
Am I satisfied with the work I did today to reach my goals?

☐ Yes ☐ No

If yes, what helped today?
If no, what can I refocus on tomorrow?

Date ___/___/___

Rate each on a scale from 1-10 (1=low, 10=high)
 Mood:___ Stress:___ Energy:___ Motivation:___
Am I satisfied with the work I did today to reach my goals?

☐ Yes ☐ No

If yes, what helped today?
If no, what can I refocus on tomorrow?

Date ___/___/___

Rate each on a scale from 1-10 (1=low, 10=high)
 Mood:___ Stress:___ Energy:___ Motivation:___
Am I satisfied with the work I did today to reach my goals?

☐ Yes ☐ No

If yes, what helped today?
If no, what can I refocus on tomorrow?

Date ___/___/___
Rate each on a scale from 1-10 (1=low, 10=high)
 Mood:___ Stress:___ Energy:___ Motivation:___
Am I satisfied with the work I did today to reach my goals?

☐ Yes ☐ No

If yes, what helped today?
If no, what can I refocus on tomorrow?

Date ___/___/___
Rate each on a scale from 1-10 (1=low, 10=high)
 Mood:___ Stress:___ Energy:___ Motivation:___
Am I satisfied with the work I did today to reach my goals?

☐ Yes ☐ No

If yes, what helped today?
If no, what can I refocus on tomorrow?

Date ___/___/___
Rate each on a scale from 1-10 (1=low, 10=high)
 Mood:___ Stress:___ Energy:___ Motivation:___
Am I satisfied with the work I did today to reach my goals?

☐ Yes ☐ No

If yes, what helped today?
If no, what can I refocus on tomorrow?

Date ___/___/___

Weekly Reflection

What emotion have I felt most often this week?

[ ]

Did I take time to notice how I was feeling before or after a big moment?

☐ YES ☐ NO

What was the moment? What did you notice. Whether or not you forgot to pay attention to how you were feeling at the time, how do you feel about it now?

[ ]

Write about a moment that challenged you mentally this week. How did you respond?

[ ]

How intense were your practices or workouts this week? Did anything shift mentally?

[ ]

Read Aloud:

I FOCUS ON WHAT I CAN CONTROL.
I AM PREPARED AND READY.

Week 52
LOOKING FORWARD

> *"The future belongs to those who prepare for it today."*
> — *Malcolm X*

This is not the end.

It is a checkpoint.

You have built habits. You have learned how to check in with yourself. You have proven that consistency matters more than motivation.

This week is about carrying that forward.

You do not need all the answers. You need direction, intention, and the willingness to keep showing up.

Whatever comes next, a new season, a new role, or a new challenge, you are more prepared than you were a year ago.

That matters.

Date ___/___/___

Rate each on a scale from 1-10 (1=low, 10=high)

MOOD: ___ STRESS: ___ ENERGY: ___ MOTIVATION: ___

Am I satisfied with the work I did today to reach my goals?

☐ YES   ☐ NO

If yes, what helped today?
If no, what can I refocus on tomorrow?

Date ___/___/___

Rate each on a scale from 1-10 (1=low, 10=high)

MOOD: ___ STRESS: ___ ENERGY: ___ MOTIVATION: ___

Am I satisfied with the work I did today to reach my goals?

☐ YES   ☐ NO

If yes, what helped today?
If no, what can I refocus on tomorrow?

Date ___/___/___

Rate each on a scale from 1-10 (1=low, 10=high)

MOOD: ___ STRESS: ___ ENERGY: ___ MOTIVATION: ___

Am I satisfied with the work I did today to reach my goals?

☐ YES   ☐ NO

If yes, what helped today?
If no, what can I refocus on tomorrow?

Date __/__/__

Rate each on a scale from 1-10 (1=low, 10=high)
  MOOD: ___ STRESS: ___ ENERGY: ___ MOTIVATION: ___

Am I satisfied with the work I did today to reach my goals?

☐ YES   ☐ NO

If yes, what helped today?
If no, what can I refocus on tomorrow?

Date __/__/__

Rate each on a scale from 1-10 (1=low, 10=high)
  MOOD: ___ STRESS: ___ ENERGY: ___ MOTIVATION: ___

Am I satisfied with the work I did today to reach my goals?

☐ YES   ☐ NO

If yes, what helped today?
If no, what can I refocus on tomorrow?

Date __/__/__

Rate each on a scale from 1-10 (1=low, 10=high)
  MOOD: ___ STRESS: ___ ENERGY: ___ MOTIVATION: ___

Am I satisfied with the work I did today to reach my goals?

☐ YES   ☐ NO

If yes, what helped today?
If no, what can I refocus on tomorrow?

Date ___/___/___

Weekly Reflection

What emotion have I felt most often this week?

[ ]

Did I take time to notice how I was feeling before or after a big moment?

☐ YES   ☐ NO

What was the moment? What did you notice. Whether or not you forgot to pay attention to how you were feeling at the time, how do you feel about it now?

[ ]

Write about a moment that challenged you mentally this week. How did you respond?

[ ]

How intense were your practices or workouts this week? Did anything shift mentally?

[ ]

Read Aloud:
I FOCUS ON WHAT I CAN CONTROL.
I AM PREPARED AND READY.

A Message to Your Future Self

This is the last time you'll be asked to write in this journal.
Based on everything you've learned and experienced over the last year, write something you think you may want or need to read later.

Something real.

Something True.

Something yours.

THIS YEAR WAS NOT ABOUT PERFECTION.

IT WAS ABOUT SHOWING UP.

YOU LEARNED. YOU EVOLVED. YOU GREW.

CARRY THIS MINDSET WITH YOU.

YOUR WORK IS NOT DONE.

YOUR STORY IS STILL BEING WRITTEN.

KEEP GOING!

www.ingramcontent.com/pod-product-compliance
Lightning Source LLC
Chambersburg PA
CBHW060518080526
44586CB00012B/530